Unbelievably Good Deals and Great Adventures That You Absolutely Can't Get Unless You're Over

50

Unbelievably Good Deals and Great Adventures That You Absolutely Can't Get Unless You're Over 50

Joan Rattner Heilman

CB

CONTEMPORARY BOOKS

Library of Congress Cataloging-in-Publication Data

Heilman, Joan Rattner.
    Unbelievably good deals and great adventures that you
absolutely can't get unless you're over 50 / Joan Rattner Heilman.
— 9th updated ed.
      p.   cm.
    Includes index.
    ISBN 0-8092-3101-8 (pbk.)
    1. Travel.   2. Discounts for the aged.   I. Title.
G151.H44   1997
910′.2′02—dc21   97-3773
                                                CIP

Cover design by Kim Bartko
Interior design by Terry Stone

15   14   13   12   11   10   9   8   7   6   5   4   3   2   1

Contents

1

Introduction to Good Deals and Great Adventures

his book is for people who love to do interesting things and go to new places—and don't mind saving money while they're at it. It is a guide to the perks, privileges, discounts, and special adventures to which you have become entitled simply because you've been around for 50 years or more.

On your 50th birthday (or on your 60th, 62nd, or 65th), you qualify for hundreds of special opportunities and money-saving offers that have lots of younger people wishing they were older. All for a couple of good reasons. First, you deserve them, having successfully negotiated your way through life's white waters.

Second, as the fastest-growing segment of the American population, you represent an enormous market of potential consumers, a fact that has become quite apparent to the business community. More than a quarter of the U.S.

population today is over 50; by 2020 that proportion is expected to increase to a third. About 1 in 8 Americans is now over 65, outnumbering teenagers for the first time in history, and the 55- to 74-year-old group accounts for 40 percent of the population. Besides, life expectancy is higher today than ever before, and most of us can expect to live a long, healthy, and active life.

Those of us over 50 control most of the nation's wealth, including half of the discretionary income, the money that's left over after essentials have been taken care of, and almost 80 percent of its financial assets. Very often, the children have gone, the mortgage has been paid off, the house is fully furnished, the goal of leaving a large inheritance is not a major concern, and the freedom years have arrived at last.

As a group, we're markedly different from previous older generations who pinched pennies and saved them all. We, too, know the value of a dollar, but we feel freer to spend our money because we're better off than our predecessors, a significant number of us having accumulated enough resources to be reasonably secure. We also are far better educated than those before us, and we have developed many more interests and activities.

And, most important, we as a group are remarkably fit, healthy, and energetic. We are in *very* good shape—and feel that way. In fact, a survey has shown that most of us feel at least 15 years younger than our chronological age.

The business community is actively courting the mature market, as we are known, because now we have the time and the money to do all the things we've always put off. Because of the recognition of our numbers, our flexible schedules, and our vast buying power, we are finally being taken very seriously. To get our attention, we are increasingly presented with some real breaks and good deals, all of which are detailed on these pages. We are also invited on trips and adventures specifically tailored to suit our interests, needs, and abilities. You will find them here too.

In this book, you will learn how to get what's coming to you—the discounts and privileges you absolutely couldn't get if you were younger:

- Discounts at hotels and motels, at car-rental agencies, on buses, trains, and boats
- Price breaks on airfares from virtually all airlines
- Colleges and universities that offer you an education for free—or nearly
- Insurance companies with discounts for people at 50 or thereabouts
- Travel adventures all over the world designed specifically for older travelers
- Clubs, trips, and services for mature singles
- Ski resorts where you can ski for half price—or for nothing
- Tennis tournaments, golf vacations, bike tours, and senior softball leagues designed for you
- And much more!

Because every community has its own special perks to offer you, make a practice of *asking* if there are breaks to which you are entitled wherever you go, from movies to museums, concerts to historic sites, hotels to ski resorts, restaurants to riverboats, in this country and abroad. Don't expect clerks or ticket agents, tour operators, restaurant hosts, even travel agents to volunteer them to you. First of all, they may not think of it. Second, they may not realize you have reached the appropriate birthday. And third, they may not want to call attention to your age, just in case that's not something you would appreciate!

Remember to request your privileges *before* you pay or when you order or make reservations, and always carry proof of age or an over-50-club membership card, or, better yet, both. Sometimes the advantages come with membership in a senior club, but usually they are available to anyone over a specified age.

To make sure you're getting a legitimate discount when you want to take advantage of your over-50 privileges away from home, call the hotel, airline, car-rental company, or tour operator and ask what the regular or normal prices are. Find out if there's a special sale going on. Then decide whether you are getting a good deal. And, most important, always ask for *the lowest available rate* at the time you plan to travel and compare that with your discounted rate. Sometimes you'll find that even better specials are available.

With the help of this guidebook, updated every year, you will have a wonderful time and save money too.

2

Travel: Making Your Age Pay Off

People over 50 are the most ardent travelers of all. They travel more often, farther, more extravagantly, and for longer periods of time than anybody else. Ever since the travel industry discovered these facts, it's been after our business.

It's fallen in love with our age group because we have more discretionary income than people of other ages and more time to spend it. Besides, we are remarkably flexible. Many of us no longer have children in school, so we're free to travel at off-peak times or whenever we feel the need for a change of scenery. In fact, we much prefer spring and fall to summer. Some of us have retired, and others have such good jobs that we can make our own schedules. We can take advantage of midweek or weekend slack times when the industry is often eager to fill space.

But, best of all, we are energetic, and we're not about to stay home too much. People over 50 account for about one-third of all domestic travel, air trips, hotel/motel nights, and trips to Europe and Africa. Nine out of ten of us are experienced travelers and savvy consumers.

Contrary to what a younger person might think, people in the mature generation aren't content with watching the action. Instead, we like to get right into the middle of it. There's not a place we won't go or an activity we won't try. Though many of us prefer escorted tours, almost half of us choose to travel independently.

Not only that, but we're shrewd—we look for the best deals to the best places. We are experienced comparison shoppers and seek the most for our money.

For all these reasons, we are now offered astonishing numbers of travel-related discounts and reduced rates as well as special tour packages and other perks. Many agencies and tour operators have designed all or at least part of their trips for a mature clientele. Others include older travelers with everyone else but offer us special privileges.

Most airlines sell senior coupon books, good for a year, that let us travel much more cheaply than other people or, instead, give those of us over 62 a 10 percent reduction on regular fares. And practically all hotel and motel chains—as well as individual establishments—now offer similar inducements, such as discounts on rooms and restaurants.

There are so many good deals and great adventures available to you when you are on the move that we'll start right off with travel.

But, first, keep in mind:

■ Rates, trips, and privileges tend to change at a moment's notice, so check out each of them before you make your plans. Airlines and car-rental agencies are particularly capricious, and it's hard to tell what they offer from one week to the next. The good deals in this guidebook are those that are available as we go to press.

■ Always ask for your discount when you make your reservations or at the time of purchase, order, or check-in. If you wait until you're checking out or settling your bill, it may be too late.

■ Also remember that discounts may apply only between certain hours, on certain days of the week, or during specific seasons of the year. Research this before making reservations and always remind the clerk of the discount when you check in or pay your fare. Be flexible when you can and travel during the hours, days, or seasons when you can get the best deals.

■ It's particularly important when traveling to carry identification with proof of age or membership in a senior club. In most cases, a driver's license or passport does the job. So, in some cases, does the organization's membership card, a birth certificate, a resident alien card, or any other official document showing your date of birth. If you're old enough for a Medicare card or Senior ID card, use that.

■ Don't always spring for the senior discount without checking out other rates. Sometimes special promotional discounts available to anybody any age turn out to be better deals. The car-rental companies and railroads, for example, are famous for this. Ask your travel agent or the ticket seller to figure out the *lowest possible available rate* for you at that moment.

■ If you belong to a senior organization, some of these bargains are yours at age 50. Others come along a little later at varying birthdays, so watch for the cutoff points. Also, in many cases, if the person purchasing the ticket or trip is the right age, the rest of the party, a traveling companion, or the people sharing the room are entitled to the same reduced rates.

3

Out-of-the-Ordinary Escapades

If you are an intrepid, energetic, perhaps even courageous sort of person who's intrigued by adventures that don't tempt the usual mature traveler, take a look at these great possibilities. They are all designed to give you tales with which to entertain your friends, relatives, and acquaintances—at least until you embark on the next one.

ALASKA WILDLAND ADVENTURES

If you're a mature traveler who wants to see Alaska up close without worrying about keeping up with a lot of 30-somethings, consider one of this outfitter's Senior Safaris. These soft adventure tours are designed to accommodate all levels of ability and stamina. The trips, starting and ending in Anchorage, are scheduled for seven or nine days in the summer months and limited to 18 participants. Lodging always includes your own private bathroom.

Adventures include rafting down the Kenai River; a yacht trip in Prince William Sound to watch whales, sea otters, glaciers, and birds; van tours through national parks and refuges; forest hikes; visits to historic bushtowns; views of grizzly bears, moose, and other wildlife; a stay at a back-country lodge in Denali National Park; and a ride on the Alaska Railroad. Mention that you belong to a recognized senior organization, and you'll get a $50 discount.

For information: Alaska Wildland Adventures, PO Box 389, Girdwood, AK 99587; 800-334-8730.

AMERICAN WILDERNESS EXPERIENCE

If you love adventurous vacations and roughing it in style, study the many offerings from AWE, an agency that's spent many years sending travelers on backcountry wilderness adventures and taking care of all the details. Its offerings are gathered from many tour operators and are open to all ages, but some are specifically designed for over-50s, and a few give discounts to seniors. Among these are a canoe trip in the Boundary Waters between Minnesota and Ontario, senior safaris in Alaska, horseback trips in Colorado or New Mexico, and a mountain sports week that combines rock climbing, horseback riding, mountain biking, and whitewater rafting in Colorado. Other trips feature special departures and itineraries for prime timers.

For information: American Wilderness Experience, PO Box 1486, Boulder, CO 80306; 800-444-0099 or 303-444-2622.

ARIZONA RAFT ADVENTURES

The Senior Archaeology Tour offered by AZRA takes you on a four-day, 27-mile raft trip down the upper San Juan River in the southwestern corner of Utah to visit some of the areas inhabited by the Anasazi Indians hundreds of years ago. While exploring the sites along the river and hearing interpretive talks about Anasazi culture, you'll see ancient ruins, artifacts, petroglyphs, pioneer trails, geological phenomena, and abundant wildlife. You'll travel in a rubber raft rowed by a guide, spend the nights at campsites on the sandy river banks, and enjoy the company of a small group from your own generation.

For information: Arizona Raft Adventures, 4050 E. Huntington Drive, Flagstaff, AZ 86004; 800-786-7238 or 520-526-8200.

GREAT ALASKA SAFARIS

The Silver Safaris, scheduled several times each summer, were created expressly by this outfitter for older travelers who seek adventure but want their comfort too. Mellower and softer than trips planned for all ages, the eight-day safaris start at the Great Alaska Fish Camp on the Kenai Peninsula where you'll stay in riverside cabins. After hikes and other adventures, plus a glacier and wildlife cruise in Prince William Sound, there's a flight to Katmai National Park to see bears and salmon, a visit to Anchorage, and a rail journey to Denali National Park to view grizzlies, moose, and other wildlife.

For information: Great Alaska Safaris, HC01, Box 218, Sterling, AK 99672; 800-544-2261.

HOSTELLING INTERNATIONAL/ AMERICAN YOUTH HOSTELS

This organization is undoubtedly probably best known for its low-cost bike and backpack trips for teenagers, but, in fact, it welcomes people of all ages. Once you become a member, you may participate in any of its "open" or "adult" adventures and book lodgings at the nearly 5,000 remarkably inexpensive HI hostels in more than 70 countries. Membership for adults costs $25 a year, but if you've reached the age of 55 you pay only $15. You will get a membership card, a guidebook listing hostels in the United States and Canada, and access to all affiliated hostels worldwide.

The hostels vary from a castle in Germany to a lighthouse in California, a former dude ranch in Colorado, and a base camp in the Alps. Most hostels have kitchens where you prepare your own meals, and a few have cafeterias.

Members may stay at any hostel in the world, including the network of urban hostels located in Washington, D.C., New York, Boston, San Francisco, Orlando, Miami Beach, New Orleans, Los Angeles, and Honolulu. One night's stay costs $8 to $22. There is no maximum age limitation for booking a bed in these wonderfully cheap lodgings and hobnobbing with other hostelers who prefer not to pay exorbitant hotel prices. Be ready, however, to sleep in a double-decker cot in a sex-segregated dormitory for six or eight people supervised by "hostel parents." Many hostels have family or couple rooms, however, that can be reserved in advance.

For information: HI/AYH, Dept. 855, 733 15th St. NW, Ste. 840, Washington, DC 20005; 800-444-6111 or 202-783-6161.

HOSTELLING INTERNATIONAL—CANADA

A network of about 75 hostels throughout the Canadian provinces, HI-Canada offers members of all ages an inexpensive night's sleep in a wide variety of places ranging from historic homes and refurbished jails and courthouses to log cabins in the mountains. Located in all major gateway cities and also in remote locations, your accommodations—shared, simple, and quite basic—cost an average of $15 (Canadian) a night. Membership costs $25 (Canadian) per year and allows you to use any HI facility worldwide.

For information: Hostelling International—Canada, 205 Catherine St., Ste. 400, Ottawa, ON K2P 1C3; 800-663-5717 (Canada only) or 613-237-7884.

MT. ROBSON ADVENTURE HOLIDAYS

For people over 50 who crave action and the wilderness, this agency plans a couple of "gentle adventures" every summer in British Columbia's Mt. Robson Provincial Park, just west of Jasper. Mt. Robson is the highest mountain in the Canadian Rockies, and the park offers spectacular scenery. The Fifty Plus Adventure is a five-night package trip for up to 14 participants that includes a guided trek, a nature tour, a marshlands canoe trip, and a gentle rafting float trip, all led by local naturalists. You sleep in heated log cabins with private bathrooms at the base camp and eat three hearty meals a day.

For information: Mt. Robson Adventure Holidays, PO Box 687, Valemount, BC V0E 2Z0; 604-566-4386.

OUTWARD BOUND

Famous for its wilderness trips to build self-confidence, self-esteem, and the ability to work as a team, Outward Bound offers many short adventure education courses specifically for adults. A few of the courses, in fact, are limited to adults over 40 or 50 and others focus on helping to make a smooth transition from career to retirement. The physical activities are challenging and participants are expected to push themselves beyond their self-imposed physical and mental limits.

The 6- to 14-day courses include backpacking in the southern Appalachians, canoeing, sailing in the Florida Keys, and backpacking in Maine or the Texas desert. You'll sleep in a tent or under a tarp and cook your own food. To participate, you must be in good health and average physical condition but you needn't be an experienced camper. *For information:* Outward Bound USA, Route 9D, R2 Box 280, Garrison, NY 10524-9757; 800-243-8520.

OVERSEAS ADVENTURE TRAVEL

OAT offers soft adventure for travelers over 50 who want new experiences in exotic and remote places all over the world and a modicum of comfort at the same time. On these adventures, you'll lodge in accommodations ranging from jungle lodges and family-run inns to classic tenting, and use unique modes of transportation such as dugout canoes, yachts, camels, minibuses, or your own feet. The trips, rated from "easy" to "demanding," move along at a leisurely pace and offer many optional side adventures. Among the current offerings from this affiliate of Grand Circle Travel are excursions to Vietnam, Thailand, Nepal, Costa Rica, Belize, the Amazon, the Serengeti, Egypt and the Nile, Turkey, New Zealand, and an expedition to Antarctica. *For information:* Overseas Adventure Travel, 625 Mt. Auburn St., Cambridge, MA 02138; 800-221-0814 or 617-876-0533.

RIVER ODYSSEYS WEST

Specializing in "magical adventures" on land and sea, ROW reserves a couple of whitewater river trips each summer for people 55 and over who prefer to travel with people their own age and, at the same time, get a 10 percent discount on the regular price. These Prime Time trips take you down Idaho's Salmon River and the Snake River on the Oregon border for three, four, or five days, floating through four spectacular volcanic canyons. You travel by day in rubber rafts powered by professional oarspersons and sleep in tents on the river's edge by night.

A wholly different trip with one departure a year reserved for mature travelers is a 12-day sailing trip along the southern coast of Turkey in a 72-foot motor-sail yacht, again at a senior discount. You'll have plenty of time for shore visits to villages, beaches, and ancient ruins.

For information: River Odysseys West, PO Box 579-UD, Coeur d'Alene, ID 83816-0579; 800-451-6034 or 208-765-0841.

SENIOR WORLD TOURS

Strictly for older travelers, many of the trips scheduled by Senior World Tours are definitely out of the ordinary. Its best-known adventure is a winter snowmobiling holiday out of Jackson Hole, Wyoming, but this company also plans walking trips in such places as France's Dordogne River Valley, the wine country of California, the Cotswolds in England, and Montana's Glacier National Park; plus bike trips in Utah's national parks and the San Juan Islands in the Puget Sound; and rafting on Idaho's Salmon River. See Chapter 13.

For information: Senior World Tours, 2205 N. River Rd., Fremont, OH 43420; 888-355-1686.

WARREN RIVER EXPEDITIONS

Warren River Expeditions offers whitewater raft trips for seniors down Idaho's Salmon River, the longest undammed river in the country—fast and wild in the spring, tame and gentle in late summer. You'll float through unique ecosystems, down the deep Salmon River Canyon, and through the Frank Church Wilderness Area, where you'll view the lush scenery and the abundant wildlife. Planned as soft adventure trips for people who are not enthusiastic about sleeping on the ground, the six-day senior trips put you up each night in comfortable backcountry lodges. Want to take the trip with your grandchildren? There is a grandparents expedition twice every summer plus a 10 percent discount for those over 50 or under 16.

For information: Warren River Expeditions, PO Box 1375, Salmon, ID 83467-1375; 800-765-0421 or 208-756-6387.

TAKE A GRANDCHILD ON VACATION

Would you like to get to know your grandchildren better? Take them on vacation. A trip with the kids is a wonderful way to get close to them, especially for families who live many miles apart and don't see one another very often. Whether it's a one-day tour of a nearby city or two weeks on an African safari, this is the kind of family togetherness that works. You can plan your own itineraries, maybe visiting places you both want to see, staying in a cottage at the beach, or going to a resort. Or you can do it the easy way and choose one of the many ready-made grandparent vacations now available.

Growing in popularity too are other multigenerational holidays, such as adventures for mothers and grown daughters, hostelers and adult children, and whole families including children, parents, and grandparents. Here are some of the current choices for a vacation with the family.

AFC TOURS

Enjoy quality time with your grandchildren without the hassles of planning and traveling on your own by getting on board one of AFC's grandparent tours. Scheduled during summer vacation are one-week trips to Walt Disney World and Epcot Center; Boston; Washington, D.C.; Charlottesville and Colonial Williamsburg; and New York City and Philadelphia. You'll have a supervised program that includes activities for both generations with a tour manager leading the way.

For information: AFC Tours, 11772 Sorrento Valley Rd., San Diego, CA 92121; 800-369-3693 or 619-481-8188.

AMERICAN MUSEUM OF NATURAL HISTORY FAMILY TOURS

This prestigious museum runs educational travel trips for children (17 and up) accompanied by parents or grandparents (or both). You and your grandchildren may choose to spend the winter holidays sailing aboard a clipper ship in the Caribbean and visiting six tropical islands. Or decide to take a trip to Ecuador and the Galapagos Islands where you'll cruise among remote volcanic islands and make the acquaintance of the unique wildlife. Other choices for family tours include an Alaska wilderness and glacier exploration, and a winter safari to Kenya for close encounters with lions, elephants, and giraffes. Groups are led by museum naturalists.

For information: Discovery Tours, American Museum of Natural History, Central Park West at 79th St., New York, NY 10024; 800-462-8687 or 212-769-5700.

ELDERHOSTEL

Elderhostel, the well-known educational travel organization for people over 55 and mates, now offers a number of intergenerational programs—some for Elderhostelers and their adult children, some for members and their grandchildren or other young friends. All of them are designed to give you a good time while you enjoy one another's company unhassled by everyday pressures. The offerings vary from season to season, but some of the recent programs have been held at Yosemite Institute in Yosemite National Park; Western Montana College in Dillon, in the shadow of the Rocky Mountains; Wolf Ridge Environmental Learning Center, in Minnesota; Atlantic Mountain Ranch, in South Dakota; Otter Creek Park, in Kentucky; and Strathcona Park Lodge, on Vancouver Island in British Columbia.

For information: Elderhostel, 75 Federal St., Boston, MA 02110; 617-426-7788. In Canada: Elderhostel Canada, 308 Wellington St., Kingston ON K7K 7A7; 613-530-2222.

FAMILYHOSTEL

FamilyHostel is an international travel and learning program for families—parents, grandparents, and children

(8 to 15)—sponsored by University of New Hampshire Continuing Education, which also runs the Interhostel program for adults over 50 (see Chapter 16). It takes families on 10-day summer trips to foreign countries where, separately and together, they attend presentations and classes led by faculty from local educational institutions, go on field trips to contemporary and historic sites, attend social/cultural events, and enjoy recreational activities for all generations. Family-style accommodations are in residence halls, university apartments, or hotels. Current trips go to Provence or Normandy in France, London, Switzerland, Vienna, and Wales. The moderate cost includes airfare, meals, accommodations, and activities.

For information: FamilyHostel, University of New Hampshire, 6 Garrison Ave., Durham, NH 03824; 800-733-9753.

GRANDEXPLORERS

GrandExplorers, recently created by the B'nai B'rith Center for Jewish Family Life, is designed to help grandparents pass on family traditions and heritage to their grandchildren, instilling Jewish values and identity in an age when family members tend to live far apart. Its major program is a 10-day vacation in Israel that includes stays in Jerusalem and Tel Aviv, a jeep tour of the Golan Heights, a camping trip with a Bedouin family for the children, camel rides, visits to historic sites throughout Israel, two nights on a kibbutz, and get-togethers with Israeli families and artists.

For information: GrandExplorers, B'nai B'rith Israel Commission, 1640 Rhode Island Ave. NW, Washington, DC 20036; 800-500-6533 or 202-857-6577.

GRANDPARENT/GRANDCHILD SUMMER CAMP

Take your grandchild to camp with you for a week this summer. The mission of this camp, led by the Foundation for Grandparenting and planned especially for families whose members don't live next door, is to bring the two generations together by giving them the time and space to be alone together, escape from the demands of the everyday world, experience the power and joy of their bond, and have fun. The site is the Sagamore Institute, a former Vanderbilt "great camp" in New York State's Adirondack Park.

In the mornings, campers engage in joint activities such as walks, berrypicking, group games, and nature art. In the afternoons, the age groups are on their own, free to choose from many recreational activities. Before dinner, grandparents meet for discussions of their own issues, and in the evenings everyone gets together for stories, campfires, singalongs, square dancing, or other activities.

For information: Sagamore Institute, Sagamore Rd., Raquette Lake, NY 13436; 315-354-5311.

GRANDPARENTS/GRANDKIDS CAMP

Every summer, the College of the Tehachapis, a unique community-based, continuing-education institution in California, joins with Elderhostel to host three six-day sleepaway camp sessions for grandparents and their grandchildren, ages 6 to 12. The two generations lodge in cottage units in one of several rustic California locations, and together they have fun fishing, boating, riding, hiking, singing, doing arts and crafts, and touring. Here's another good opportunity to enjoy your grandchildren on your own at a modest cost.

For information: COTT, PO Box 1911-61, Tehachapi, CA 93581; 805-823-8115.

GRANDTRAVEL

Grandtravel was the first agency to offer special trips for grandparents and their grandchildren so they can share the pleasures of traveling together. Grandtravel's series of itineraries, scheduled for normal school breaks, aims to appeal to both generations. It includes trips to Washington, D.C., or Alaska; tours through the American Southwest or New England; a Hawaiian tour; African safaris; visits to China, Australia, Ireland, England, Scotland, Switzerland, and France; a tour of national parks; tours of London and Paris via the Chunnel; barge trips in Holland and more! Grandtravel will also arrange for independent grandparent/grandchild travel, family groups, or school-sponsored groups.

Actually, you don't have to be a grandparent to take the trips—aunts, uncles, cousins, godparents, and other surrogate grannies are welcome. Ranging from 7 to 18 days, the tours, led by teacher-escorts, include good hotels with recreation facilities, transportation by motorcoach with rest stops every two hours, games, talks, music on the buses, and a travel manual for every tour. Each trip provides time for the older folks and the children to be alone with their own age group. The kids may go roller skating and dine on fried chicken—supervised, of course—while the grandparents do something grown up, such as going to a gourmet restaurant for dinner.

For information: Grandtravel, The Ticket Counter, 6900 Wisconsin Ave., Chevy Chase, MD 20815; 800-247-7651 or 301-986-0790.

IRISH FESTIVAL TOURS

For a visit to your Irish roots, gather up your grandchildren (or nieces, nephews, or other young friends) this summer and take them on a 10-day tour that includes Dublin, Avoca, Waterford, Killarney, the Ring of Kerry, and Galway. You'll learn about the folklore and traditions of the Irish people; visit castles, villages, and museums; listen to storytellers; go pony trekking; see a working dairy farm; learn traditional dances; and otherwise enjoy a respite just for you and the grandkids. Most activities include both generations, but some separate events are planned as well.

For information: Irish Festival Tours, PO Box 169, Warminster, PA 18974; 800-441-4277.

OUTDOOR VACATIONS
FOR WOMEN OVER 40

For a multigenerational adventure trip, check out the offerings of this unusual agency that specializes in vacations for groups of women who love the outdoors. Several of its weekend trips out of Boston are designed specifically for mothers, daughters, grandmothers, granddaughters, aunts, and nieces who want to spend time together. At least two generations must be represented, with one participant over 40 and the other over 21. Among the current multigenerational opportunities are three-day windjammer cruises off the coast of Maine and hiking trips in New Hampshire.

For information: Outdoor Vacations for Women Over 40, PO Box 200, Groton, MA 01450; 508-448-3331.

RASCALS IN PARADISE

Specializing in family vacations for parents and children, Rascals in Paradise also invites grandparents and grandchildren to go along on its adventure trips to such places as Mexico and the Caribbean, the Bahamas, Europe, New Zealand, Thailand, Australia, the Canadian Rockies, Africa, the Galapagos Islands, Hawaii, Alaska, and ranches in the West. All group trips, three to six families per group, include escorts who plan activities for the older children and baby-sitters for the little ones. This agency will plan independent vacations, too, as well as family reunions and other multigenerational celebrations.

For information: Rascals in Paradise, 650 Fifth St., Ste. 505, San Francisco, CA 94107; 800-872-7225 or 415-978-9800.

RFD TOURS

If you're looking for new traveling companions, consider your grandchildren. The trips for the two generations scheduled by this agency always feature special attractions for the kids and mature activities for the grannies. Recent itineraries, all in the summer, have included an American Heritage Tour that takes the travelers from Philadelphia to Washington, D.C.; a narrow-gauge train trip through the Colorado Rockies; a week in New York City; a pilgrimage to Branson; and a tour of the West's most spectacular national parks. Come the winter holidays, there's a week-long trip to southern California that ends up at the Rose Parade in Pasadena.

For information: RFD Tours, 1225 Warren Ave., Downers Grove, IL 60515; 800-365-5359 or 630-960-3974.

SHOTT'S WALKS IN THE WEST

You and your grandchildren over 18 are invited on this intergenerational walking trip in Alaska scheduled every August. You'll be based at Kennicott Glacier Lodge in a former ghost town in Wrangell–St. Elias National Park. You will hike the glaciers and walk through the forests, visit the colorful town of Talkeetna, in the shadow of Mount McKinley, and view the wildlife in Denali National Park.

For information: Shott's Walks in the West, PO Box 51106, Colorado Springs, CO 80949; 719-531-9577.

SIERRA CLUB

A couple of remarkably inexpensive summertime vacations for grandparents and their grandchildren, led by experienced volunteers, are recent arrivals among the Sierra Club's famous outings. One of these outings is a laid-back and relaxed holiday, while the other is a rugged adventure recommended only for grandmas and grandpas in very good physical condition.

The first is a five-day stay at the Sierra Club's own rustic lodge near Donner Pass, in California's Sierra Nevadas. The outing is designed for people between 5 and 95, and all activities are optional. You lodge in rather spartan rooms, eat hearty meals, and enjoy yourselves doing such things as hiking, strolling, climbing to the top of Donner Peak, taking the tram to the top of Squaw Valley, picnicking at Donner Lake, fishing, swimming, visiting historic sites, and singing around the campfire.

The more rigorous outing for the two generations is a four-day backpacking trip in California's Carson-Iceberg Wilderness. This one is definitely not for couch potatoes—grandparents must have previous backpacking experience and must be able to hike with full packs at high elevations. You'll hike to a base camp carrying your personal gear plus commissary gear and food, set up camp, help cook and clean up, and spend your days hiking, fishing, swimming, and exploring.

For information: Sierra Club Outing Dept., 85 Second St., San Francisco, CA 94105; 415-977-5522.

VISTA TOURS

The Grandparent/Family tours from Vista Tours schedule two grandparent/grandchildren itineraries every summer. A 10-day Old West tour takes you to many U.S. and Canadian national parks; and a five-day bus trip to Reno and Lake Tahoe includes the Ponderosa Ranch, Virginia City, and Donner Summit. Activities are planned for the two generations separately and together, with a goal of bringing everyone closer through shared experiences. The groups are small and the activities varied.

For information: Vista Tours, 1923 N. Carson St., Ste. 105, Carson City, NV 89701; 800-248-4782.

WARREN RIVER EXPEDITIONS

Every summer, this tour operator offers two Grandparents/ Grandkids raft trips down Idaho's Salmon River, a great way for the two generations to spend time together. You stay in rustic lodges along the way. Refer to Warren River Expeditions earlier in this chapter for more about this adventure.

For information: Warren River Expeditions, PO Box 1375, Salmon, ID 83467-1375; 800-765-0421 or 208-756-6387.

4

Cutting Your
Costs Abroad

he most enthusiastic voyagers of all age groups, Americans over 50—one out of three adults and a quarter of the total population—spend more time and money on travel than anybody else, especially when it comes to going abroad. It's been estimated that more than 4 out of every 10 passport holders are at least 55 years old. And there's hardly a country in the world today that doesn't actively encourage mature travelers to come for a visit, because everybody has discovered that they are travel's biggest potential market.

Because you are currently being hotly pursued, you as well as the local residents can take advantage of many good deals in other lands. Railroad systems in most European countries, for example, offer deep discounts to seniors that are especially valuable if you plan an extended stay in one place. This chapter gives you a rundown on these and other ways to cut your European holiday costs, especially if you are planning your trip on your own. For the U.S. and Canada, see Chapter 9.

But, first, keep in mind:

■ Always ask about senior savings when you travel on trains, buses, or boats anywhere in the world. Do the same when you buy tickets for movies, theater, museums, tours, sightseeing sites, historic buildings, and attractions. Don't assume, simply because you haven't heard about them or the ticket agent hasn't mentioned them, that they don't exist. They are becoming more and more common everywhere.

■ Some countries require that you purchase a senior card to take advantage of senior discounts, but most require only proof of age, usually in the form of a passport.

■ Always have your necessary identification with you and be ready to show it. Occasionally you may need an extra passport photograph.

■ For specifics on a country's senior discounts, call its national tourist office. Or call Rail Europe (800-438-7245), which represents most European railways, for information about train passes.

■ Your passport may be required along with your rail pass while you are in transit, so keep it with you.

■ Rail passes, including many national passes, sold in the U.S. and Canada can be bought from any travel agency or directly from Rail Europe. The one-country passes that must be purchased abroad are available at major rail stations within that country. Be prepared to show your passport.

EUROPE BY RAIL

Rail passes make the going cheaper in Europe, especially if you travel with a companion or a group, and they're easier than buying tickets as you go. Besides, some of them offer senior discounts. It's not a simple matter to sort them all out, however. Some are multinational, good for travel in more than one country. Others are valid only within the borders of one country; these are usually designed for residents but useful to tourists as well. Most passes are available in two different versions: a flexipass which permits travel for a specified number of days within a certain time period, and the consecutive-day pass that is valid on any day within a certain period. Many are not available overseas and must be purchased on this side of the Atlantic before you go. Others may only be purchased in the country that issues them.

FINDING A DOCTOR OVERSEAS

Before you leave on a trip to foreign lands, it would be wise to send for a list of physicians all over the world who speak English or French, have had medical training in Great Britain, the U.S., or Canada, and have agreed to reasonable preset fees. When you join the free nonprofit International Association for Medical Assistance to Travellers (IAMAT), you will get a membership card entitling you to services and its prearranged rates, a directory of physicians in 125 countries and territories, a clinical record to take along with you, advice on immunizations and preventive measures, and information on sanitary conditions in 450 cities.

For information: IAMAT, 417 Center St., Lewiston, NY 14092; 716-754-4883.

EURAILPASS AND EUROPASS

The Eurailpass gives you free unlimited first-class train travel in Hungary and on all the major railways of Western Europe except Britain's. There is no senior discount on this pass, but it is worth considering if you plan to cover many miles in many countries. On the other hand, if you are visiting just one country, you'd probably do better with that nation's senior discounts or national pass. Available for various numbers of days up to three months, the Eurailpass also entitles you to free or discounted travel on many buses, ferries, steamers, and suburban trains. If you are traveling with at least one other person, you can get a Eurail Saverpass or Eurail Saver Flexipass, an even better deal.

The Europass, less expensive, is another option. It is good for unlimited first-class train travel any time within a two-month period in five western European countries (France, Germany, Italy, Spain, and Switzerland). Other countries may be added with a surcharge.

None of these passes is sold in Europe but must be purchased before you leave home. And none gives seniors a special break.

For information: Rail Europe, 2100 Central Ave., Boulder, CO 80301; 800-4-EURAIL (800-438-7245).

SCANRAIL 55+ PASS

Also sold only on this side of the Atlantic, Scanrail gives you unlimited travel in Denmark, Finland, Norway, and Sweden. If you're over 55, buy the Scanrail 55+ Pass, giving you the same privileges, but for less than younger adults pay. For details, see Scandinavian Countries later in this chapter.

For information: Rail Europe, 2100 Central Ave., Boulder, CO 80301; 800-4-EURAIL (800-438-7245).

EUROSTAR: THE CHANNEL TUNNEL

Eurostar offers 12 round trips a day through the tunnel that goes under the English Channel connecting Paris and Brussels with London. The senior fares—you're eligible if you're over 60—are 20 percent less than the regular adult fares for both first class and standard class. They are also unrestricted and refundable.

For information: Rail Europe, 800-EUROSTAR or 800-4-EURAIL.

COUNTRY-BY-COUNTRY TRAVEL DEALS

AUSTRIA

In Austria, women at age 60 and men over 65 may buy half-fare passes valid on the Austrian Federal Railways and the bus system of the Federal Railways and the Postal Service (except on municipal subways, trolleys, and buses). To get the pass you must first buy a Railway Senior Citizens ID available at all rail stations and some major post offices in Austria as well as Frankfurt and Cologne, Germany, and Zurich, Switzerland. You must have proof of your age (your passport) and an extra passport photo. The card is good for the calendar year and currently costs about $27. It is not available in the United States but may be obtained before your trip by mail from Austria or purchased at central rail stations in Austria or Germany.

In Vienna, pick up a Vienna Card at your hotel desk

or a tourist information office. Available to all ages, it costs about $18 and gives you unlimited travel on all forms of public transportation within the city limits for three days. It also gets you reduced admission to the leading museums, attractions, concerts, and sightseeing tours of the city for four days as well as some shopping discounts. In Innsbruck, you may buy a Museum Card that gives you access to 11 museums; and in Salzburg, the Salzburg Card gains you admission to local transit, sightseeing attractions, museums, the zoo, and the casino.

For information: Austrian National Tourist Office, PO Box 1142, New York, NY 10108-1142; 212-944-6880.

BELGIUM

Travelers over the age of 60 and companions over 55 may buy Golden Railpasses, available only in Belgium, that give them six single journeys on the Belgian railway network for 1,990 Belgian francs (about $66 at this writing), first class, or 1,290 francs (about $43), second class. If you plan only a short trip, however, a better choice may be the Belgian Half-Fare Card (570 francs), available to anyone any age and valid for a month. It allows you to travel on all trains for half price.

For information: Belgian National Tourist Office, 780 Third Ave., New York, NY 10017; 212-758-8130.

BERMUDA

Every year Bermuda dedicates the month of February to visitors over the age of 50. During Golden Rendezvous Month, there are daily special events, activities, lectures, and tours designed for them. Many hotels offer special packages and rates, and free bus tours of the island are offered. A coupon book good for discounts at retail stores and sight-seeing attractions plus two free ferry and bus tokens per person, can be picked up at the Visitors Service Bureau in Hamilton.

For information: Bermuda Department of Tourism, 310 Madison Ave., New York, NY 10017; 800-223-6106.

FRANCE

Once you possess the Carte Vermeil, available only in France at main train stations, you may buy tickets on the French National Railroad (SNCF), first or second class, at half price if you are over 60. The Carte Vermeil Quatre Temps costs about 140 francs at this writing, and allows for four half-fare rail trips within a year; the Carte Vermeil Plein Temps, about 270 francs, gives you unlimited rail travel at half price for a year. Be sure to have your passport or driver's license handy.

You may buy railroad tickets at 50 percent off only for trips made during the "period bleue" or non-rush hours: from noon on Saturday until 3 P.M. on Sunday, and from Monday noon until Friday noon. At other times you will get a 20 percent discount on your fare. There is no discount on the Paris suburban train network.

Using the more expensive Carte Vermeil Plein Temps card, you may also get a 30 percent reduction any day of the week on tickets from France to most other European countries.

If you are flying within France on the domestic airline Air Inter, inquire about reduced fares offered to travelers over 60. These fares, usually 40 to 60 percent off the full fares, are available on most flights in non-peak hours. And, of course, always check out the senior discounts at museums, movies, concerts, and other cultural events. *For information:* French Government Tourist Office, 444 Madison Ave., New York, NY 10022; 212-838-7800.

GREAT BRITAIN

You'll get some really good bargains in the U.K. because the British favor "the very good years" and offer senior discounts and special rates on almost everything from railroads to hotels (especially off-season), buses, museums, day cruises, theaters (sometimes only for matinees), and historical sites. Ask if there is an OAP (Old Age Pensioners) rate wherever you go. For travel information and useful tips before you go, the British Tourist Authority is your source. *For information:* British Tourist Authority, 551 Fifth Ave., New York, NY 10176; 800-GO 2 BRIT (800-462-2748) or 212-986-2200.

In Britain, where virtually every town may be reached by train, it pays to consider buying a rail pass if you're not renting a car for your explorations. U.S. travelers over 60 get 15 percent (Canadians get 20 percent) off the cost of first-class rail travel in England, Scotland, Wales, and Northern Ireland when they buy a BritRail Senior Pass. It comes in two versions: the BritRail Senior Flexipass, good for unlimited travel on any 4, 8, or 15 days in a one-month period, and the BritRail Senior Classic Pass that permits first-class travel on consecutive days. You may buy this pass for 8, 15, or 22 days, or for one month. Both of these passes must be purchased before you leave home. They are not accepted in Ireland or on special excursion trains. With both plans, you may hop on and off the trains as often as you like along the way.

By the way, here's a good deal if you're traveling with your children or grandchildren. Buy a Senior Pass (or regular adult pass) and one accompanying child (5 to 15 years old) gets a free pass of the same type and duration. Additional children going with you get half off the adult pass price, and children under 5 travel free.

If you're spending time in London, a London Visitor Travelcard (get it there) is worth considering because it gives you, whatever your age, unlimited travel on London Transport's subway and bus network for a choice of 3, 4, or 7 days. It includes an underground transfer from Healthrow International Airport to central London and travel on many British Rail trains in the London area.

Another option is the Senior Railcard that's available only in the U.K. Designed for residents but useful for visitors who spend considerable time in Britain, it is good for a year for a flat fee of about $25. It reduces your rail fares about 30 percent. Check it out with British Rail when you get there.

And don't leave home without a Great British Heritage Pass that allows unlimited entry into more than 500 castles, palaces, manor homes, and gardens in England, Scotland, Wales, and Northern Ireland. Get it from BritRail.
For information: BritRail, 1500 Broadway, New York, NY 10036; 800-677-8585 or 212-575-2667. In Canada: 800-555-2748.

If you want to travel by bus, look into a Tourist Trail Pass. This gives you unlimited travel aboard National Express motorcoaches in England, Scotland, and Wales for 3 to 15 days within a 30-day period. It's a good deal in any case, but once you are over 50, you may buy it at a discount of about 20 or 25 percent off the regular adult fare. The pass may be purchased in the U.S. by mail or phone. It is not available in the U.K.

For information: National Express, PO Box 299, Elkton, VA 22827; 540-298-1395.

Another useful pass is the London Museum White Card that may be purchased in London at participating museums, galleries, and hotels. It gives you admission to a dozen museums. And the London for Less card provides substantial discounts at over 200 attractions, shows, concerts, tours, hotels, shops, and restaurants, plus a map and a guidebook. One card is good for two to five people for four consecutive days. Buy it here before you go or, in London, pick one up at the British Hotel Reservation Center in Victoria Station.

For information: Call London for Less at 800-244-2361.

GREECE

Here, if you are 60, male or female, you may buy a Hellenic Railways pass that's good for five single train trips within Greece. When you've used up your five trips, you may travel at half price. Valid for one year, the pass may be purchased at any major railroad station in Greece. The only hitch: there are some blackout periods when the card doesn't do the trick—from July 1 to the end of September, plus the 10 days before and after Easter and Christmas.

For information: Greek National Tourist Organization, 645 Fifth Ave., New York, NY 10022; 212-421-5777.

HONG KONG

Because so many visitors to Hong Kong are members of the older generation, the Hong Kong Tourist Association offers its *Mature Travellers Guide*, a booklet with useful information and practical advice, plus a list of special discounts on transportation, dining, and shopping for people over the age of 60. With it comes the Silver Plus Card to use for discounts, complete with instructions.

For information: Hong Kong Tourist Association, 590 Fifth Ave., New York, NY 10036-4706; 212-869-5008.

IRELAND

Many hotels in the Republic of Ireland offer senior discounts, especially off-peak, so make it a policy to inquire about them when making your reservations. In most cases, you must be 65 to qualify. Theaters (midweek), national monuments, and historic sites give you price reductions too. Always ask.

No doubt you'll be spending time in Dublin, so it would be wise to buy a Dublin Supersaver Card that takes 25 percent off the admission fees to museums, castles, and other cultural sites in that city. It currently costs 15 pounds (about $24) for an adult pass, but if you are 65 you'll get it for 12 pounds (about $19). It is available at the Dublin Tourism Center and at participating sites in the city, or you may buy it here before you go.

For information: Irish Tourist Board, 345 Park Ave., New York, NY 10154; 800-223-6470 or 212-418-0800.

ITALY

The Carta d'Argenta (Silver Card), which currently costs about $27 and is valid for a year, entitles anyone over 60, tourist or resident, to a 20 percent discount on all rail travel in Italy. You can buy it at railroad stations in Italy at the special windows (Biglietti Speciali) and must show it when you buy your tickets to get the lower fares. It is not available on this side of the Atlantic. This card will obviously save you money if you plan to travel extensively in Italy, but the Flexi-Rail Pass or Italian Railcard, available at any age, which may be purchased both in the U.S. or Italy, may prove to be a better value for shorter stays with less mileage. Check out all of your choices before making a decision.

For information: CIT Tours, 342 Madison Ave., New York, NY 10173; 800-223-7987 or 212-697-2100.

LUXEMBOURG

Anybody over 65 pays half fare on trains and buses. Just show proof of age when you buy your tickets.

For information: Luxembourg National Tourist Office, 17 Beekman Pl., New York, NY 10022; 212-935-8888.

NETHERLANDS

Whenever you go to museums, attractions, cultural and historic sites, or on tours in Holland, always ask if there is a senior discount because people over 60 are usually given a break on admission fees. Have your passport handy to prove your age.

If you'll be staying in the Netherlands for at least a few months, it makes sense to buy a 60+ Pass that provides you with a 40 percent discount on Dutch Railways trains, except during rush hours, on holidays, or Mondays and Fridays. A bonus: you also get seven free travel days which may be used once every two months, with the seventh day good any time. The pass costs 99 guilders (currently about $66) at railroad stations and is valid for a year.

In Amsterdam, consider buying an Amsterdam Culture & Leisure Pass, good for a year, at Schiphol Airport or a VVV Amsterdam Tourist Office in the city. The pass is not age-oriented, but it will give you coupons for free admission to many museums, a free canal cruise, a guided tour at a diamond-cutting house, and discounts on some restaurants and other cruises. Cost at this writing is about $19.

For information: Netherlands Board of Tourism, 225 N. Michigan Ave., Chicago IL 60601; 888-GO-HOLLAND (888-464-6552).

NEW ZEALAND

Travelers over 60 are entitled to a Golden Age discount of 30 percent off the standard adult fares on all Tranz Scenic Trains in this country. Buy your tickets at the railroad station.

For information: New Zealand Tourism Board, 501 Santa Monica Blvd., Santa Monica, CA 90401; 800-388-5494 or 310-395-7480.

PORTUGAL

You may travel on trains within Portugal at a 30 percent discount off the regular adult fare if you are at least 65 years old and ready to pull out your passport to prove it.

For information: Portuguese National Tourist Office, 590 Fifth Ave., New York, NY 10036; 212-354-4403.

SCANDINAVIAN COUNTRIES

If you are a mature traveler, Scandinavia has some good deals for you. First of all, you may travel in four Scandi-

navian countries—Denmark, Sweden, Norway, and Finland—less expensively than other people.

One way is to take advantage of the Scanrail 55+ Pass,
which must be purchased in the U.S. before you go. This
gives you a pass at discounted prices, if you are 55, for unlimited travel by train in all four countries. You may buy
the pass for five days (to be used within 15 days), for 10
days (to be used within a month), or for a month of consecutive days, allowing you to travel wherever you like on
the national rail networks. Bonuses (some of which may
constitute usage of a travel day) include free passage on several water crossings, half price on several cruise lines, 25
percent discount on certain ferries, and discounts from 10
to 30 percent on hotel room rates during the months of
June, July, and August.
For information: Call your travel agent or Rail Europe at
800-4-EURAIL (800-438-7245).

Now here are the current country-by-country opportunities for mature travelers:

Denmark: Here you may buy "65-Tickets" for reduced
train fares in first or second class every day of the week,
with the fare even less on "cheap days" (Monday through
Thursday and Saturday).

Sweden: If you buy the Reslust Card in Sweden, you
will get a 25 percent discount on all train journeys over 50
miles, on Tuesdays, Wednesdays, Thursdays, and Saturdays. And you may also take advantage of discounts in dining cars, special summer rates, and more. The card, which
currently costs everyone else about $18 (U.S.), costs you
(at 65 or older) only $6.

Norway: Norway's offer is half price for a train ticket, first or second class, any time, anywhere. For this, however, you or your spouse must be 67. Also at 67, you become eligible for a discount on Norwegian Coastal Voyages (except in June or July) and, at 60, half price on Color Line cruises to England and the Continent (see Chapter 5).

Finland: The Finnish Senior Citizen Card, available for about $9 (U.S.) at railroad or bus stations, entitles you at age 65 to half fare on trains and 30 percent off on bus trips that are at least 80 kilometers one way. The Silja Line, ships that serve North Sea ports, offers junior rates to seniors.

Also look into the Scandinavian BonusPass. It is not age-oriented but gives discounts of up to 50 percent off the rates at more than a hundred first-class hotels during the summer season and on weekends all year.

Travelers to cities in Scandinavia should consider buying city cards that offer discounts and savings on everything from transportation to car rentals and tours. Get the cards at tourist offices, airports, or hotels. They are available for Copenhagen, Odense, and Aalborg, Denmark; Helsinki and Tampere, Finland; Oslo, Norway; Stockholm, Gothenburg, and Malmo, Sweden.

For information: Scandinavian National Tourist Offices, 655 Third Ave., New York, NY 10017; 212-949-2333.

SWITZERLAND

The Swiss Hotel Association will provide, for the asking, a list of over 450 hotels that participate in the "Season for Seniors," giving reduced rates to women over 62 and men over 65 (if you are a couple, only one of you must be the required minimum age). The only catch is that in most cases the lower rates do not apply during peak travel periods, including the summer months.

Although the following travel passes are not just for mature travelers but are available to everyone, they are worth noting because they may save you considerable money on fares:

The first is the Swiss Pass, useful if you are planning to do extensive traveling within the country because it allows you unlimited trips on the Swiss Travel System, including most private and mountain railroads, lake steamers, and most postal motorcoaches, public tramways, and buses in 30 cities. It also lets you buy excursion tickets to mountaintops at 25 percent off. Buy it for 8 days, 15 days, or a month.

With the Swiss Flexi Pass you may travel three days within a 15-day period.

And then there's the Swiss Card. Valid for one month, it gives you one free trip from any entry point to your destination within Switzerland and return. In addition, with the Card you may purchase an unlimited number of tickets on all scheduled services by train, postal coach, or lake steamer at half price.

The travel passes are available in the U.S. through your travel agent or Rail Europe. In Switzerland, they are sold at many railroad stations and airports upon showing your passport.

For information: Swiss National Tourist Office, 608 Fifth Ave., New York, NY 10020; 212-757-5944. Or Rail Europe, 2100 Central Ave., Boulder, CO 80301; 800-4-EURAIL (800-438-7245).

5

Trips and Tours for the Mature Traveler

A few enterprising organizations and travel agencies now cater only to the mature traveler. They choose destinations sure to appeal to those who have already seen much of the world, arrange trips that are leisurely and unhassled, give you congenial contemporaries to travel with and group hosts to smooth the way, and provide many special services you never got before. They also give you a choice between strenuous action-filled tours and those that are more relaxed. In fact, most of the agencies offer so many choices that the major problem becomes making a decision about where to go.

Options range from cruises in the Caribbean or the Greek Isles to grand tours of the Orient, sight-seeing excursions in the United States, trips to the Canadian Rockies, theater tours of London, African safaris, and snorkeling vacations on the Great Barrier Reef off Australia. There's just no place in the world where over-50s won't go.

Among the newer and most popular trends are apartment/hotel complexes in American and European resort areas, as well as apartments in major cities. Here you can stay put for as long as you like, using the apartment as a home base for short-range roaming and exploring.

To qualify for some of the trips, one member of the party must meet the minimum age requirement, while the others may be younger.

TRIPS FOR THE MATURE TRAVELER
AFC TOURS

Specializing in escorted tours designed for mature travelers, AFC schedules trips to all the most popular destinations in the U.S. and Canada and some in other countries. Not only that, but you are picked up at your home and transported to and from the airport. Domestic tours take you to such places as the national parks, Washington, D.C., Branson, Nashville, New York City, Savannah, and New Orleans. International adventures include New Zealand and Australia, Costa Rica, London, Bangkok, and Hong Kong. Other choices: cruises, steamboating, train tours, holiday tours, and grandparent trips. In other words, almost anything you want. Special for singles: If you sign up four months in advance and a roommate cannot be found to share your room, you need not pay a single supplement.
For information: AFC Tours, 11772 Sorrento Valley Rd., San Diego, CA 92121; 800-369-3693 or 619-481-8188.

AJS TRAVEL CONSULTANTS

The AJS 50 Plus Club plans its many trips, all leisurely and escorted, for the older generation. Among the current offerings are tours of Israel, spa vacations in Italy, stay-put vacations in Swiss resort towns, lakeside vacations in Switzerland, Caribbean and Alaskan cruises, and tours of the Imperial Trail: Prague, Vienna, and Budapest. Land travel is by motorcoach. Annual family membership fee for the club is $25.

For information: AJS Travel Consultants, 177 Beach 116th St., Rockaway Park, NY 11694; 800-221-5002 or 718-945-5900.

AMERICAN JEWISH CONGRESS

AJC sponsors trips all over the world, from China to Greece, Australia, and the British Isles, but specializes in tours that take Jewish travelers to Israel or on Jewish Heritage Expeditions for extensive explorations of their history. Led by

HOW TO KEEP POSTED ON PERKS

Here's a newsletter with an attitude! *The Over-50 Thrifty Traveler* celebrates the positive side of getting older, keeps track of the perks, aims to save you money, and insists that being over 50 can be lots of fun. For "baby boomers and young-thinking seniors of all ages," the eight-page monthly newsletter is full of money-saving suggestions and useful advice.

For information: The Over 50 Thrifty Traveler, PO Box 8168, Clearwater, FL 34618; 800-532-5731 or 813-447-4731.

scholars, the two-week expeditions, all of which tend to at-tract mature travelers, currently cover four areas where Jews once flourished: Eastern Europe (Lithuania, Poland, Czech Republic, Hungary), Spain, Provence (France), and Morocco. Some departure dates of these history-laden trips are designated for single travelers over the age of 55.

Among AJC's many tours of Israel, "Israel Slow & Easy" is tailored specifically for older travelers. This is a 15-day trip that takes you all over this tiny country, always mov-ing at a leisurely pace. Again, at least one departure a year is reserved for singles over 55.

For information: American Jewish Congress, 15 E. 84th St., New York, NY 10028; 800-221-4694 or 212-879-4588.

BACKROADS TOURING CO.

Designed especially for adults over 50, the tours planned by BackRoads Touring Co. take groups of no more than 12 participants on explorations of England, Scotland, Wales, Ireland, France, Spain, Italy, or Portugal, along the back roads to out-of-the-way places. You'll travel by minivan with a knowledgeable local guide for one or two weeks, lodge in historic houses, inns, or bed and breakfasts, and won't spend a fortune. These are leisurely tours with plenty of time to explore. You'll stay several nights in the same lo-cation, spend time with local residents. You may even help plan the itinerary. Add-on stays in London are available, too, and so is a four-day trip to Wales out of London. What's more, if you mention this book, you will get a discount.

For information: BackRoads Touring Co., British Network Ltd., 594 Valley Rd., Upper Montclair, NJ 07043; 800-274-

8583 or 201-744-5215. In Canada, contact Golden Escapes, 75 The Donway West, Ste. 910, Don Mills, ON M3C 2E9; 800-668-9125 or 416-447-7683.

CIE TOURS INTERNATIONAL

An agency whose trips go only to Ireland and England, CIE offers motorcoach tours and fly/drive vacations, many of which come with a 55 and Smiling Discount. This means that on certain departure dates you get $55 per person off the cost of the trip if you are 55 or older.

For information: CIE Tours International, 100 Hanover Ave., Cedar Knolls, NJ 07927; 800-CIE-TOUR (800-243-8687) or 201-292-3438.

COLLETTE TOURS

The worry-free vacations for the mature population from Collette Tours, one of the oldest escorted-tour companies in the U.S., include over 100 itineraries in more than 50 countries from South America to the Orient, Europe, Africa, and our own continent. It even offers an around-the-world tour every year. Its trips move at a relaxed pace, put you up in deluxe and first-class hotels, and provide experienced tour guides to see that everything goes well. In Denmark, Scotland, Portugal, Spain, Israel, and Austria, the agency's new "Hub and Spoke" programs feature many days in one place so you don't have to keep packing and unpacking your bags. Meanwhile, you make day excursions to see the sights of the area.

For information: Collette Tours, 162 Middle St., Pawtucket, RI 02860; 800-832-4656.

CORLISS TOURS

The Stay-Put Tours by Corliss are planned with older travelers in mind—you fly to your destination, check into your hotel, hang up your clothes, and stay put, never packing your bags again until it's time to go home. Meanwhile, you go on sightseeing adventures by motorcoach and explore the area in depth. Each tour carries along a tour director who makes all the arrangements and shepherds the group around. Plenty of time, too, to relax and explore on your own. Destinations include Atlanta, Orlando, Washington, D.C., New York, Philadelphia, San Antonio, Seattle, Denver, Colorado Springs, Nashville, New Orleans, Montreal, Toronto, Calgary, and Vancouver. Each tour lasts a week, but you may link two or more trips as you like. This agency also organizes tours, many of them Stay-Puts, over the Thanksgiving and Christmas holidays, taking you to resorts, festivals, and popular vacation destinations such as Washington, D.C., Williamsburg, New Orleans, Branson, Myrtle Beach, and Scottsdale.

For information: Corliss Tours, 436 W. Foothill Blvd., Monrovia, CA 91016; 800-456-5717.

DELTA QUEEN STEAMSHIP CO.

If you want to revisit the old days, take a nostalgic cruise on the *Mississippi Queen*. As you steam up the river from New Orleans on a "World War II Vacation" cruise, you'll look back and reminisce, sharing stories with illustrious veterans, listening to all your favorite old songs, dancing to the biggest big band sounds of the day, and celebrating at the Stage Door Canteen Party. Another option is one of Delta

Queen's "Year That Was" cruises. You may choose the cruise that celebrates 1942, 1943, 1945, 1946, or 1948. You'll recapture the joys and sorrows of those important years while you share your memories and dance the night away with the big band sounds.

For information: Delta Queen Steamship Co., 30 Robin Street Wharf, New Orleans, LA 70130-1890; 800-543-1949.

ELDERTREKS

If you insist on viewing the world through bus windows or on sleeping in five-star hotels, stop reading now, because on ElderTreks' trips you'll be doing a lot of walking and maybe you'll sleep in a tribal village. ElderTreks is a program of off-the-beaten-track trips for people 50 and older (and younger companions) who are in reasonably good

CHOOSING A PLACE TO RETIRE

Lifestyle Explorations conducts two-week group tours in countries that it considers to be ideal retirement destinations. You may choose tours of Costa Rica, Portugal, Uruguay and Argentina, Honduras, Ireland, Canada's Maritime Provinces, Venezuela, or Hungary, combining a vacation with on-site seminars with local professionals and Americans already living there. Each area has been rated according to cost of living, taxes, health care, climate, safety, friendliness, government stability, and cultural opportunities.

For information: Lifestyle Explorations, 101 Federal St., Ste. 1900, Boston, MA 02110; 508-371-4814.

physical condition, capable of walking at a comfortable pace in tropical conditions. Featuring exotic adventures to relatively remote places in the world, it stresses cultural interaction, physical activity, and nature exploration. However, trekking routes are chosen with older hikers in mind and groups are limited to 15. Trekking portions of the trips are optional and you may choose to substitute a guesthouse-based itinerary.

Accommodations for the city portions of the tours are in clean, comfortable tourist-class hotels and guesthouses chosen for charm and location. Accommodations on the adventure portions may be on the floor of a house in a tribal village or camping under a canopy of trees in the jungle, but you can always count on having an air mattress to sleep on. Guides, cooks, and porters are part of the package. Destinations include Thailand, Borneo, Vietnam, Laos, Samoa, Sumatra, Java, Bali, China, Tibet, Nepal, India, Turkey, Ecuador and the Galapagos Islands, Costa Rica, Bolivia, Peru, New Zealand, and Belize.

For information: ElderTreks, 597 Markham St., Toronto, ON M6G 2L7; 800-741-7956 or 416-588-5000.

EVERGREEN TOURS

A Canadian company based in British Columbia, Evergreen Tours sells escorted tours created exclusively for mature travelers. Professional tour directors accompany every trip, taking care of all the details so you are free to relax and enjoy yourself. You will travel by deluxe motorcoach and stay in first-class accommodations. Your choice of tours ranges from a 19-day exploration of the Big Sky Country or the Northwest Territories to a 27-day trip through Australia and New Zealand and a 2-week cruise through the Panama Canal. Also vacations over the holidays in British Columbia, the Canadian Rockies, and the U.S. Northwest.

For information: Evergreen Tours, 555 W. Hastings St., Vancouver, BC V6B 4N4; 800-663-1478.

GALAXY TOURS

If you are an armed forces veteran, how would you like to revisit the scenes of your wartime experiences? Galaxy Tours' series of "nostalgic journeys" takes groups of veterans, their families, and friends back to the lands where they spent their tours of duty in World War II and the Vietnam War. The most popular tour retraces the route of the American forces from England into Normandy during the invasion of France on D-Day and after. Another trip lets you return to the China-Burma-India theater to see the places you served as a GI and the many special sights you didn't have a chance to appreciate then. You may revisit the sites of the Battle of the Bulge, or visit Germany if you were stationed there after 1946. Veterans of the war in Vietnam, too, are offered a trip that takes them back to the scenes they once knew so well.

For information: Galaxy Tours, PO Box 234, Wayne, PA 19087-0234; 800-523-7287 or 610-964-8010.

GO AHEAD VACATIONS

Go Ahead Vacations, a division of EF that has specialized for many years in intercultural exchange and educational travel, plans an endless array of escorted worldwide tours and cruises exclusively for older travelers. On this continent, tours range from 9 days in the Canadian Rockies to 16 days in the top national parks. In Europe, there's a 19-day land-and-sea tour of Greece, 17 days in Norway, and trips to every other country you've ever wanted to see. Hotels are first class or superior. All tours are led by professional tour directors, usually natives of the country you are visiting. A multitude of cruise vacations is also among the offerings from this agency.

If you ask for a roommate, you'll get one or have your single supplement reduced by half. All tours are sold directly to travelers through catalogs.

For information: Go Ahead Vacations, 1 Memorial Dr., Cambridge, MA 02142; 800-242-4686. Ask for the free booklet, *Travel Tips.*

GOLDEN AGE FESTIVAL TRAVEL

Another agency that caters to the mature crowd, this one offers escorted tours to everywhere from Wildwood (New Jersey), Myrtle Beach, Nashville, Maine, and New York to the national parks, Las Vegas, Europe, Greece, and Hawaii. Plus plenty of cruises. All packages are escorted and include accommodations, meals, and just about everything else.

In addition, Golden Age Festival offers a real innovation—drive tours for individual travelers, allowing them to take advantage of group discounts that make the trips remarkably inexpensive. On these, all on the East Coast, you drive yourself to your destination—for example, Wildwood, Ocean City, Myrtle Beach, Newport and Mystic Seaport, Hilton Head, Williamsburg—and join others traveling on their own for meals, entertainment, and tours.

For information: Golden Age Festival Travel, 5501 New Jersey Ave., Wildwood Crest, NJ 08260; 800-257-8920 or 609-522-6316.

GOLDEN AGE TRAVELLERS

This over-50 club's specialty is discounted cruises to just about everywhere in the world, but it offers land trips at group rates as well. When you join the club ($10 a year or $15 per couple), you will receive a quarterly newsletter with listings of upcoming adventures, discounts, and bonuses on major cruise lines. Other inducements are tour escorts on every venture and credits against the transportation costs to the airport on certain trips. Single travelers may choose to be enrolled in the "Roommates Wanted" list to help them find companions to share cabins and costs. For members in the San Francisco and Sacramento areas, there are one-day excursions and meetings where you may meet fellow travelers.

Especially intriguing to mature travelers are this agency's long-stay trips. On these, you stay put—for example, in Spain, Portugal, Guatemala, Australia, Costa Rica, or Argentina—at the same hotel for two or three weeks, and, if you wish, take short side trips. The packages include air, hotel, and sometimes meals.

For information: Golden Age Travellers, Pier 27, the Embarcadero, San Francisco, CA 94111; 800-258-8880 or 415-563-2361.

GOLDEN ESCAPES

Golden Escapes for the 50-Plus Traveller are tours run by a Canadian agency that offers all-inclusive escorted tours in

Canada, the U.S., and Europe as well as three-week tours of such exotic places as Greece, Egypt, Cyprus, Turkey, and Morocco. It also has long-stay programs where you lodge in an apartment or a hotel in a resort area—perhaps Portugal's Algarve, Newport Beach, Palm Springs, or the island of Crete—and take excursions by day, highlighted by parties, happy hours, entertainment, and other activities. In addition, Golden Escapes is the representative in Canada for BackRoads Touring Co., which takes you on minicoach tours of England, France, Scotland, or Portugal. Other sightseeing adventures for over-50s include trips to popular U.S. destinations, including Washington, D.C., Myrtle Beach, and Savannah.

For information: Golden Escapes, 75 The Donway West, Ste. 910, Don Mills, ON M3C 2E9; 800-668-9125 or 416-447-7683.

GRAND CIRCLE TRAVEL

Grand Circle caters to people over 50 and plans all of its trips exclusively for them. The first U.S. company to market senior travel, it has escorted over 600,000 Americans all over the world. The agency specializes in Live Abroad Extended Stays. Sign up and you will live in an apartment, villa, or house in a foreign country for anywhere from 2 to 26 weeks at a moderate cost. At the moment, you may choose to live in the British Isles, southern France, Switzerland, Austria, Turkey, Italy, Greece, Spain, Portugal, Morocco, Costa Rica, or Mexico. You may decide to be on your own during your stay or to use the services of the onsite program director who is always available to help you plan your days.

Traditional escorted tours are on the menu, too, taking you to destinations all over the world on international or domestic land trips as well as cruises and cruise/tours. Grand Circle's Discovery Series is another option, offering educational/travel trips to interesting foreign destinations where you become immersed in the local culture, history, art, environment, and politics. You'll visit local families, take language lessons, learn to cook regional foods, attend lectures, and learn all about the country you are visiting.

Single travelers with GCT pay only half of the single supplements on most trips when they have requested a travel roommate and none is available. And on a few Live Abroad departure dates, they pay no supplements at all.

GCT donates a part of its profits to a nonprofit foundation which funds humanitarian and environmental projects around the world. It is also associated with Overseas Adventure Travel. See Chapter 3.

For information: Grand Circle Travel, 347 Congress St., Boston, MA 02210; 800-248-3737 or 617-350-7500. Ask for the free booklet, *101 Tips for Mature Travelers.*

IDYLL, LTD.

The nontraditional "untours" of Europe planned by Idyll fly you to the country of your choice, escort you to your own private apartment where you'll stay for two or four weeks (or more), provide you with guidance along the way, and map out suggested itineraries for explorations of the countryside on your own. The idea is to provide a home abroad, usually an apartment in a private home, and opportunities to spend time with local people. Round-trip air and ground transportation in the form of rail passes or rental cars is included.

For information: Idyll, Ltd., PO Box 405, Media, PA 19063; 610-565-5242.

MAYFLOWER TOURS

Many of Mayflower's travelers are "55 or better," so the pace of its tours is leisurely and rest stops are scheduled every couple of hours. You travel by motorcoach, stay in good hotels or motels, and eat many of your meals together. All trips are fully escorted by tour directors who make sure all goes well. If you are a single traveler and request a roommate at least 30 days before departure, you'll get a roommate or a room to yourself at the regular double rate. Tours go almost everywhere in the United States and Canada, including national parks of the Southwest, the Canadian Rockies and Pacific Northwest, French Canada, Branson and the Ozarks, New England and Cape Cod, Hawaii, and New York. Foreign destinations include Australia, Mexico, Switzerland, Spain, and Israel, while cruises take you to the Caribbean, the Panama Canal, Alaska, Europe, or the coast of New England.

For information: Mayflower Tours, 1225 Warren Ave., Downers Grove, IL 60515; 800-323-7604 or 630-960-3430.

MIDLIFE ADVENTURES

If you're hankering for a bit of adventure and want to travel with a small companionable group of contemporaries, consider the 17-day tour of New Zealand offered by Midlife Adventures. Scheduled for departures during New Zealand's summer—October through mid-April—you'll have moderately paced outdoor experiences as you travel all over the North and South Islands seeing the sights and visiting five national and two maritime parks. Owned by "a middle-aged couple" and led by middle-aged guides, this agency will take you sailing, whitewater rafting, sea kayaking, cave rafting, glacier walks, bush walks, scenic flights, sightseeing, and hiking, for which you need no previous experience but must be in good physical shape.

For information: Midlife Adventures, 2817 Wilshire Blvd., Santa Monica, CA 90403; 800-528-6129 or 310-998-5880.

PLEASANT HAWAIIAN HOLIDAYS

Pleasant's Makua Club Holidays are special packages for vacationers over the age of 55, at a choice of more than 45 hotels and condos on four Hawaiian islands. Nothing to join, no dues to pay, and only one person per room needs to be 55. You get discounted room rates, complimentary room upgrades, and a $25 certificate per room to use

---

MEXICAN PREVIEW

Barvi Tours, a California travel company, presents a 5-night series of seminars in Guadalajara plus tours for those who are contemplating retirement in Mexico. You can then go on a group visit to the areas that interest you, and learn about health facilities, housing, culture, immigration, and other relevant matters.

For information: Barvi Tours, 11658 Gateway Blvd., Los Angeles, CA 90064; 800-824-7102 or 310-475-1861.

when you buy an optional event, activity, or excursion.
For information: Pleasant Hawaiian Holidays, 2404 Towns-
gate Rd., Westlake, CA 91361; 800-2-HAWAII (800-242-
9244).

RFD TOURS

Created many years ago to arrange visits between American and foreign farmers, and then to organize flower and
garden tours, RFD Travel now plans a wide range of U.S.
and international tours and cruises every year specifically
for mature travelers, including a series of trips designed especially for travelers to enjoy with their grandchildren. All
hosted, the trips stress cultural heritage events, personal
contacts with people in foreign countries, knowledgeable
tour managers, and an easy pace.
For information: RFD Tours, 1225 Warren Ave., Downers
Grove, IL 60515; 800-365-5359 or 630-960-3974.

SAGA HOLIDAYS

Founded in England in 1951, Saga plans trips exclusively
for travelers over 50 (and their younger traveling companions). It offers an astonishing variety of vacations from fully
escorted coach tours of any place on earth you've ever
wanted to go, to cruises and safaris, educational tours, walking tours, and all-inclusive winter resort stays. Also grand
tours of Europe, cruise-and-coach tours in Greece, holidays
in Turkey, cruises along the Alaska coast, among the Greek
islands, or in the waters off China and Vietnam. Saga's all-
inclusive resort holidays are designed to let you live a while
in one place—perhaps Portugal, Spain, or Sicily—where
you settle into your resort hotel for a relaxing, affordable hol-

iday that includes entertainment, activities, and excursions.

Here's good news for solo travelers: Saga now schedules departures for singles only on some of its holidays plus many more vacations with affordable or no-cost single supplements. See Chapter 6 for more information.

Saga also offers two educational travel programs. One is Smithsonian Odyssey Tours which, in partnership with the famed Smithsonian Institution, gives you a wide choice of learning adventures guided by experts in their fields, from investigating the mysteries of Egypt's ancient temples or the Mayan culture of the Incas to unraveling the puzzles of Machu Picchu and discovering Moorish castles in Spain and Portugal.

The Road Scholar program offers travel-study itineraries, each with a special theme such as classical Greece, Iceland's geology and history, the paintings and palaces of St. Petersburg, again with lectures by experts from academic or cultural institutions.

For information: Saga Holidays, 222 Berkeley St., Boston, MA 02116; 800-343-0273. Smithsonian Odysseys: 800-258-5885. Road Scholar Programs: 800-621-2151.

SCI/NATIONAL RETIREES OF AMERICA

This agency, which began decades ago with trips to the Catskills resorts, now offers a long list of group tours for seniors that range from one-day outings to 45-day world cruises. The land tours—5-day jaunts by air to Las Vegas are its specialty—depart midweek, transport you by motorcoach, and take you to such places as New Orleans, Quebec, Niagara Falls, the Poconos, Orlando, Nashville, or New York.

For information: SCI/National Retirees of America, 343 Merrick Ave., East Meadow, NY 11554; 800-427-7062 or 516-481-3939.

TRAFALGAR TOURS

With its escorted motorcoach trips, Trafalgar Tours caters to older travelers who want to see Europe and Great Britain without concern for problems and arrangements. You'll have organized sightseeing and activities, as well as plenty of time to do your own thing. All tours include a professional escort, first-class hotels, sightseeing, transfers, breakfast, and several dinners. If you are traveling alone, you'll be matched with an appropriate roommate.

For information: Trafalgar Tours USA, 11 East 16 St., New York, NY 10010-1402; 800-854-0103 or 212-725-7776. Ask for the free brochure, *Tour Talk.*

VALUE WORLD TOURS

On certain Value World Tours trips to central and eastern Europe, anybody over the age of 55 gets 10 percent off the regular price. The hosted or escorted motorcoach tours transport you to a choice of destinations that include Russia, Ukraine, Estonia, Latvia, Lithuania, Poland, Hungary, Czech Republic, Bulgaria, and more, where you'll sleep in four-star hotels. Also available with senior discounts are river cruises in Russia and Ukraine with stops at ports of call along the way.

For information: Value World Tours, 17220 Newhope St., Fountain Valley, CA 92708; 800-795-1633 or 714-556-8258.

VANTAGE DELUXE WORLD TOURS

Vantage features upscale tours for mature travelers and has already escorted more than a quarter of a million over-50 tourists around the world on land tours and cruises. Accommodations are always deluxe and explorations are leisurely and relaxed, so there is plenty of time to see and savor the sights. All trips are led by tour directors who see to it that everything—from ticketing and baggage handling to check-ins, meals, and tips—is taken care of for you. Among Vantage's most popular tours are a Rhine River cruise, a trip through the Panama Canal, a visit to China and the Yangtze River, an exploration of Ireland, or the countries of Eastern Europe. Plus longer, more exotic tours such as a 33-day tour around the world.

If you are traveling alone and want a roommate, a compatible companion will be found or half the single supplement on land programs will be waived.

For information: Vantage Deluxe World Tours, 111 Cypress St., Brookline, MA 02146; 800-322-6677. Ask for the free booklets, *99 Travel Tips for Mature Travellers* and *Health Guide for Older Travellers.*

VISTA TOURS

Another agency providing escorted tours almost exclusively for the mature set, Vista Tours plans leisurely trips with plenty of stops and ample time to enjoy the points of interest and relax too. You travel on comfortable motorcoaches with escorts who deal with the reservations, transfers, luggage, meal arrangements, and all other potentially problematic situations. Destinations, although mainly in the U.S., also include Canada, France, the Far East, Australia, and New Zealand. A highlight every year is a five-day trip over the New Year's holiday to California where you'll see the Pasadena Rose Parade and attend a New Year's Eve party with a big band and a celebrity show. If you're a woman who doesn't have a dancing partner or wants a better one, you may take your turn whirling around the floor with one of the gentleman hosts who always accompany the group.

For information: Vista Tours, 1923 N. Carson St., Ste. 105, Carson City, NV 89701; 800-647-0800.

CRUISING THE HIGH SEAS

Cruises have always appealed to the mature crowd. In fact, most sailings abound with people who are at least several decades out of college. So you are sure to find suitable companionship. However, never sign up for a vacation at sea without shopping around for a discount because you rarely have to pay the advertised rate. Work with your own travel agent or call a discount cruise agency to search out the best deals available when and where you want to travel.

In the meantime, for starters, here are some senior specials designed especially for you.

BALLROOM DANCERS WITHOUT PARTNERS

Are you a single person over 50 who loves to dance? Look into the many cruises scheduled every year by Ballroom Dancers Without Partners, an agency that caters to older solo travelers who love dancing more than anything. Both beginner and accomplished dancers get a chance to learn new steps during the day, and dance before dinner and after the evening's entertainment. One male host, an excellent dancer, goes along for every five passengers in the group. BDWP will arrange cabin shares so you can avoid the single surcharge. Both big bands and Latin rhythms are featured, and itineraries take you everywhere from the Caribbean to Alaska.

For information: Ballroom Dancers Without Partners, 1449 NW 15th St., Miami, FL 33125; 800-778-7953 or 407-361-9384.

BERGEN LINE

The cruises in Scandinavia of Color Line, Silja Line, and Norwegian Coastal Voyages, all exclusively represented in the U.S. by Bergen Line, offer special discounts to older travelers. Color Line, Norway's largest cruise passenger company that cruises the North Sea and travels to England and the Continent, gives travelers over 60 and a companion half-price fares on many of its trips. Silja Line, with vessels serving Finland, Sweden, Estonia, and Germany, gives passengers over 65 the same reduced fares it offers teenagers. And Norwegian Coastal Voyages, with ships that take you along the Norwegian coast from Bergen to Kirkenes, north of the Arctic Circle, takes $170–$220 per person off the round-trip fares for seniors over the age of 67 (except in June and July).

For information: Bergen Line, 800-323-7436 or 212-319-1300.

MERRY WIDOWS DANCE CRUISES

Designed for solo women from 50 to 90 who love to dance but don't have partners, the Merry Widows Dance Tours runs many cruises every year to such places as the Caribbean, the Orient, Alaska, Greece and the Mediterranean, and the South Pacific. The trips range from 7 days to 18. Sponsored by the AAA Auto Club South, the cruises take along their own gentleman hosts, one professional dancer for every five women. Each woman receives a dance card that rotates her partners every night throughout the cruise, whether she's a beginner or a polished dancer. The men are also rotated at the dinner tables so everyone gets the pleasure of their (platonic) company. You don't have to be a widow and you don't even have to know the cha-cha to have fun on these trips.

Merry Widows also operates tours at a number of major resorts, in such settings as the Cloister in Georgia's Sea Islands and Sanibel Harbor Spa Resort in Florida. Out-of-the-country resort destinations include European capitals, the Greek Isles and Turkey, Tahiti, Hawaii, and the Caribbean.
For information: Call your travel agent or contact Merry Widows Dance Tours, 1515 N. Westshore Blvd., Tampa, FL 33607; 800-374-2689.

CARNIVAL CRUISE LINES

If you're smart, you belong to AARP for its discount program. That now includes a savings of $100 per stateroom on new individual bookings in the high-end categories of cabins on Carnival's cruises of seven days or longer, or $50 per stateroom on shorter cruises. A discount certificate is

required and may be used at any travel agency, but many restrictions apply.
For Information: Carnival Cruise Lines, 800-CARNIVAL. Or AARP, 800-887-3529, for a certificate.

COSTA CRUISES

Passengers may take an additional 10 percent off the fares already discounted for bookings made at least 90 days prior to sailing date when at least one occupant of the stateroom is 60 years old.
For information: Costa Cruises, 800-327-2537.

HOLLAND AMERICA LINE

Members of AARP can book an outside stateroom on a Holland America Line cruise or Alaska cruise tour of seven days or longer and save $100 per stateroom, or $50 on a shorter cruise. A discount certificate is required and may be used at any travel agency, but many restrictions apply.
For Information: Holland America Line, 800-426-0327. Or AARP, 800-887-3529, for a certificate.

PREMIER CRUISE LINES

At 55, you and a companion who shares your stateroom get a 10 percent discount in the high season and 15 percent in the low on all of the three- and four-night cruises aboard the Big Red Boats sailing from Port Canaveral in Florida to Nassau and Port Lucaya, Bahama. The discount also applies to the seven-night packages that combine cruises with Orlando theme park vacations.

Keep your eyes open, too, for the Seniors Specials

scheduled every fall. These are even cheaper and feature big band music and ballroom dancing, gentleman hosts as dance partners, receptions, guest speakers, bridge tournaments, and more. Grandchildren may go along, too.

For information: The Big Red Boat, 800-726-5678.

ROYAL CARIBBEAN CRUISE LINE

Check with your travel agent to find out when this popular cruise line will be offering one of its special deals for seniors, because the cost on these sailings, scheduled in off-peak seasons, is always less than the lowest standard discounted rates. If one passenger in your cabin is over the age of 55 and books passage early, your party gets the same deal.

For information: Royal Caribbean Cruise Line, 800-327-6700.

ROYAL HAWAIIAN CRUISES

These day cruises—some of them luncheon or dinner cruises—take you along exclusive routes for snorkeling, exploring, whale watching, and sightseeing among the Hawaiian Islands. You are entitled to hefty discounts off the retail prices after you have reached the age of 55, so be sure to ask for them when you make your reservations.

For information: Royal Hawaiian Cruises, 800-852-4183.

CRUISE ESCORTS WANTED

Because single men of a certain age are mighty scarce among the traveling population, especially onboard ship, a growing number of cruise lines offer free travel or inexpensive travel to carefully chosen unattached men over 45—in some cases, over 65—with excellent social and dancing skills. These "gentlemen hosts"—usually retired professionals—encourage mingling among the passengers, serve as dancing or dining partners, make a fourth for bridge, act as escorts for shore trips, and generally socialize—without favoritism or romantic entanglements, we are assured—with the single women on board.

There are stringent screening procedures and many more applicants than positions, so don't be surprised if you are not encouraged to apply. Hosts must provide their own wardrobes and, in some cases, pay a fee to the placement agency for every week at sea.

American Hawaii Cruise Lines takes two dancing hosts on each of its trips all year except in the summer months, and even more on its Big Band cruises. On this cruise line that provides weekly seven-day cruises to four islands in Hawaii, the hosts, who are knowledgeable about the islands, mingle with the guests and help the single passengers enjoy their voyages and shore excursions.

For information: Working Vacation, 610 Pine Grove Ct., New Lenox, IL 60451; 815-485-8307.

Commodore Cruise Line's ship, *Enchanted Isle*, which sails every Saturday from the Port of New Orleans to Montego Bay in Jamaica, Grand Cayman, and Cozumel and Playa del Carmen in Mexico, takes at least two male dance hosts on every cruise. Single, over 50, retired or semi-retired businessmen, their job is to attend all dance lessons and to dance with passengers to live music each night of the seven-night voyage.

For information: Tom Karp Associates, 1999 University Drive, Coral Springs, FL 33071; 954-341-9400.

Crystal Cruises, whose worldwide cruises aboard the *Crystal Harmony* carry four hosts per trip, look for personable social hosts over the age of 65 who are great dancers and enjoy keeping older single women passengers entertained both on board and ashore.
For information: Entertainment Dept., Crystal Cruises, 2121 Avenue of the Stars, Los Angeles, CA 90067.

Cunard's cruises aboard *Queen Elizabeth 2*, the *Vistafjord*, the *Sagafjord*, and the *Royal Viking Sun* carry along four to ten friendly gentleman hosts between the ages of 45 and 70. Their job is not only to whirl around the dance floor with women who need partners but to act as friendly diplomats who help passengers get to know one another. A knowledge of foreign languages is a plus.
For information: Working Vacation, 610 Pine Grove Ct., New Lenox, IL 60451; 815-485-8307.

The Delta Queen Steamship Co., which makes about 50 cruises a year up and down the Mississippi River, taking you back in time aboard huge paddlewheelers, employs mature and responsible male hosts, assigning two to each trip on the *Mississippi Queen* and four to each Big Band cruise. Their job is to dance with the single women aboard, organize activities, and help everyone enjoy the voyage.
For information: Working Vacation, 610 Pine Grove Ct., New Lenox, IL 60451; 815-485-8307.

Holland America Line recruits retired professionals with good social skills to act as hosts on its "grand voyages," a world cruise, and a two-month voyage to Australia and New Zealand. Usually four hosts go along on each trip.

For information: Entertainment Dept., Holland America Line, 300 Elliott Ave. West, Seattle, WA 98119.

Merry Widows Dance Cruises offers many cruises and land tours for single, widowed, or divorced women who were born to dance. Accompanying them are gentleman hosts (one for every five women) to serve as dance partners.
For information: Merry Widows Dance Tours, 1515 N. Westshore Blvd., Tampa, FL 33607; 800-374-2689.

Orient Lines whose ship, the *Marco Polo,* sails to New Zealand and Australia, the Far East, Africa, India, and the Mediterranean, takes three or four male hosts along on most cruises to act as dance and dinner partners for the women aboard who don't have dancing partners.
For information: Working Vacation, 610 Pine Grove Ct., New Lenox, IL 60451; 815-485-8307.

Royal Cruise Line has a roster of screened 50-plus men to act as unofficial hosts on its cruise ships. With four to eight hosts aboard each ship, these congenial fellows spend their evenings whirling around the dance floor, doing their best to see that solo women travelers have a good time.
For information: Host Program, Royal Cruise Line, 1 Maritime Plaza, Ste. 1400, San Francisco, CA 94111.

Silversea Cruises has introduced gentleman hosts aboard the sister ships *Silver Cloud* and *Silver Wind.* The hosts' job is to dance, mingle, and mix, making sure all guests have an enjoyable voyage.
For information: Working Vacation, 610 Pine Grove Ct., New Lenox, IL 60451; 815-485-8307.

Sun Lines takes several professional hosts on all of its cruises aboard the *Stella Solaris.* Their assignment is to dance with all the women who love to dance but haven't brought partners along with them.

For information: Host Program, Sun Line Cruises, 1 Rockefeller Plaza, New York, NY 10020.

6

Singles on the Road

ots of people over 50 love to travel but don't have anybody to do it with. If you're single, single once again, or have a spouse who isn't the traveling kind, there's no need to give up your dreams of faraway places simply because you don't want to travel alone. There are many organizations and packagers ready to come to your aid. Some offer special trips for mature singles where you mingle with others on their own, and some help match you up with a fellow traveler—of the same or opposite sex— who is also looking for a compatible person with whom to share adventures, a room, and expenses. Traveling with another person is usually more enjoyable and certainly less expensive than going alone because you share double accommodations, thereby avoiding the usual single supplement which can be substantial.

MATCHMAKERS
TRAVEL COMPANION EXCHANGE

TCE specializes in matching up single travelers so they may go on joint adventures together and always have roommates to share expenses and experiences. Managed by travel expert Jens Jurgen, who works very hard at making compatible connections, Travel Companion Exchange is the largest, most enduring, and most successful matchmaking service. In fact, it has recently absorbed several other travel-partner services, including Golden Companions, a club that specialized in seniors.

Members receive bulky bimonthly newsletters packed with travel tips and helpful advice plus long listings of people (TCE now has close to 3,000 active members) who are seeking new friends and/or travel partners of the same or opposite sex. For more information about those who seem to be good possibilities, you send for Profile Pages about them (meanwhile, others send for yours) so you may judge their suitability for yourself. You do your own matchmaking. Jurgen suggests you talk by telephone, correspond, meet, and, even better, take a short trip together before setting out on a major adventure.

Currently, you may join TCE at an introductory fee of $99 for eight months, using a credit card if you wish. By the way, you don't have to join to subscribe to the *TCE Newsletter* (without listings) for $39 per year. Always many pages, it is a gold mine of detailed, up-to-the-minute travel information useful to all inveterate travelers. It has been named by *Newsday* as one of the three best general travel newsletters in the country.

For information: Travel Companion Exchange Inc., PO Box 833, Amityville, NY 11701; 800-392-1256 or 516-454-0880. Send $5 for a sample newsletter.

PARTNERS FOR TRAVEL

Partners for Travel, with a few hundred members, provides a matchmaking service for independent single travelers, most of whom are in the Miami area. For a membership of $60 a year or $36 for six months, you receive an informative eight-page bimonthly newsletter and profiles of fellow members who are looking for travel mates. Contacts and travel arrangements are then up to you. The club also organizes and escorts tours, spa vacations, and cruises for single, divorced, or widowed men and women over 45. All singles, members or not, may participate in these events as well as an annual National Singlefest, a week of social networking. *For information:* Partners for Travel, PO Box 560337, Miami, FL 33256; 800-866-5565 or 305-661-1878.

SAGA HOLIDAYS

Saga, well known for its holidays for mature travelers, has just initiated singles-only departures with no single supplements on several of its itineraries. Not only that, but there are now no supplements for solo participants on more than a score of its other tours all over the world, and, on several vacations, the single supplements are under $100.

Saga Holidays also attempts to match travelers with roommates, if requested—another way to eliminate additional single charges and provide companionship.

Its third option for singles is the Penfriends and Partnerships program, part of the Saga Club. This is a personals column in the club's quarterly newsletter, *Saga Magazine*, for members who wish to correspond with other members or find companions for future travel. If you join the club (annual fee: $49.95), you will also get a discount on airline senior coupon books and notice of last-minute specials, credits, and upgrades.

For information: Saga Holidays, 222 Berkeley St., Boston, MA 02116; 800-343-0273.

TOURS FOR SOLO TRAVELERS

Several tour operators and agencies specializing in escorted trips for people in their prime will try to find you a roommate (of the same sex) to share your room or cabin so you will not have to pay a single supplement. And, if they can't manage to find a suitable roommate, they will usually reduce the supplement even though you'll have your own private room. Some run singles trips as well. In any case, keep in mind that you'll hardly have time or opportunity to be lonely on the typical escorted tour run by these agencies. If you are planning an extended stay in just one location, however, you may have more need for company.

For more about the tour operators listed below, see Chapter 5. Other companies may offer the same singles-matching service, though they don't make a point of it, so always ask about it if you're interested.

BALLROOM DANCERS
WITHOUT PARTNERS

This agency specializes in cruises for single men and women who like to travel and love to dance. No need to take a partner along because dance hosts see to it that you never lack for attention. See Chapter 5.

For information: Ballroom Dancers Without Partners, 1449 NW 15th St., Miami, FL 33125; 800-778-7953 or 407-361-9384.

GOLDEN AGE TRAVELLERS

An over-50 club, Golden Age Travellers will enroll you in its "Roommates Wanted" list if you wish help in finding a companion with whom to share the costs and the fun. See Chapter 5 for more information about this club.

For information: Golden Age Travellers, Pier 27, The Embarcadero, San Francisco, CA 94111; 800-258-8880.

GRAND CIRCLE TRAVEL

Grand Circle, which concentrates on over-50 travel packages, tries to match singles with appropriate roommates if they request them. If there are none at hand, you will be charged only half the single supplement for your own room on most trips. And on several of its Live Abroad Vacations departure dates, you will not pay the single supplement at all. See Chapter 5 for more about Grand Circle.

For information: Grand Circle Travel, 347 Congress St., Boston, MA 02210; 800-248-3737 or 617-350-7500.

MATURE TOURS

Mature Tours "for youthful spirits over 50" specializes in travel for members of the mature population who wish to roam the world with other people—singles or couples—their own age. A division of Solo Flights, it will try to find you a roommate if you want to avoid the single supplement. Recent trips have included a show tour of London, a visit to Israel or Spain, all scheduled for the winter holidays; Alaska cruises in the summer; a cruise through the Panama Canal; or four days doing the town in New York, a paddlewheeler steamboat cruise on the Mississippi out of New Orleans, and nine days in Costa Rica.

For information: Mature Tours, 10 Greenwood Lane, Westport, CT 06430; 800-266-1566 or 203-256-1235.

MAYFLOWER TOURS

Another travel operator with mature travelers as its focus, Mayflower will also get you a roommate if you like or, if that's not possible, absorb the cost of the single-room supplement. You'll then pay the regular twin rate.

For information: Mayflower Tours, 1225 Warren Ave., Downers Grove, IL 60515; 800-323-7604 or 708-960-3430.

MERRY WIDOWS DANCE TOURS

If you are a single woman over 50 who was born to dance, consider a trip with the Merry Widows. Known for its cruises, it also has land tours that transport you to exciting places on this continent and abroad, not only to dance but also to see the sights. If you're traveling alone, you'll be assigned a roommate if you want one. See Chapter 5 for more.

For information: Merry Widows Dance Tours, 1515 N. Westshore Blvd., Tampa, FL 33607; 800-374-2689.

PARTNERS FOR TRAVEL

A matchmaking agency for singles, Partners for Travel also organizes and escorts trips, tours, and cruises for solo travelers over 45 years old. More information earlier in this chapter.

For information: Partners for Travel, PO Box 560337, Miami, FL 33256; 800-866-5565 or 305-661-1878.

SAGA HOLIDAYS

A tour company with trips exclusively for people over 50, Saga Holidays will try to find a roommate for you on its escorted tours and cruises so you won't have to pay the single supplement. It guarantees a roommate for land holidays, or no extra charge if one can't be found. See Chapter 5.

For information: Saga Holidays, 222 Berkeley St., Boston, MA 02116; 800-343-0273.

A WEEK IN THE SUN

The Forever Young program from Club Med offers travelers over 55 a discount of $150 per person per week, or $20 per day, at five Club Med locations chosen because they meet at least two of these criteria: an interesting excursion program, a top golf course at the village or nearby, intensive sports programs, good shopping, and comfortable accommodations without a lot of stairs and no hill climbing. The participating locations include Columbus Isle (San Salvador, Bahamas), Caravelle (Guadaloupe), Paradise Island (Nassau), Sandpiper (Florida), and Cancun (Mexico).

For information: Call your travel agent or 800-CLUB MED (800-258-2633).

SOLO FLIGHTS

This agency makes it its business to know about the best tours, cruises, packages, groups, and rates for single people of all ages, and will suggest where to go on short holidays or lengthy vacations here or abroad. It represents major tour operators and cruise lines and also offers its own package trips, some marketed by its affiliate, Mature Tours, exclusively for older travelers. One call or letter and you can find out what's out there that might possibly interest you. In return for the consultation, the agency hopes to do your booking.

For information: Solo Flights, 10 Greenwood Lane, Westport, CT 06880; 800-266-1566 or 203-256-1235.

HOOK-UPS FOR SOLO RVers

RVers who travel alone in their motor homes or vans can hook up with others in the same circumstances when they join one of the groups mentioned below. All of the clubs provide opportunities to travel together or to meet at campgrounds on the road, making friends with fellow travelers, and having fun.

LONERS OF AMERICA

LOA is a club for single campers who want to travel together. Established in 1987, it currently has 29 chapters throughout the country and well over 1,000 active members from their 40s to their 90s, almost all retired and widowed, divorced, or otherwise single. Many of them live year-round in their motor homes or vans, and others hit the road only occasionally. They camp together, rally together, caravan together, often meeting at special campgrounds that cater to solo campers.

A not-for-profit member-operated organization, the

club sends you a membership directory twice a year and a lively monthly newsletter that alerts you to campouts and rallies all over the country. The chapters organize their own events as well. Currently, dues are $30 a year plus a $5 registration fee for new members.

For information: Loners of America, PO Box 3314, Napa, CA 94558; 888-805-4562.

LONERS ON WHEELS

A camping and travel club for mature single campers, Loners on Wheels is not a lonely hearts club or a matchmaking service, but simply an association of friends and extended family. With about 65 chapters located throughout the United States and Canada, it now has a membership of about 2,800 unpartnered travelers. The club schedules hundreds of camping events during the year, at sites that are usually remote and/or primitive and cost little. A monthly newsletter and an annual directory keep everyone up to date and in touch. Annual dues at this writing are $36 U.S. and $45 Canada, plus a one-time enrollment fee of $5.

For information: Loners on Wheels, PO Box 1355, Poplar Bluff, MO 63902. Ask for a free sample newsletter.

RVing WOMEN

A club for women who travel in recreational vehicles, RVing Women was designed to be a support group for women alone on the road. It provides a forum through which they can make contacts and travel connections with other women on their own, perhaps linking up to travel and caravan together. For a $39 annual membership fee, members receive a bimonthly newsletter full of technical and travel information, a directory of members (many of whom encourage overnight stays with information on hookups and assistance), and a free U.S. trip-routing service. More than 50 regional rallies are scheduled every year all over the U.S., and caravans move out together every so often for week-long trips throughout Alaska, Canada, and Mexico. There are local happenings among members in many parts of the country as well.

For information: RVing Women, PO Box 1940, Apache Junction, AZ 85217; 602-983-4678.

7

Airfares:
Improving with Age

O ne thing that improves with age—yours—is airfare. Almost every airline now offers senior coupon
books that are probably the single best airfare deal
going. The basic idea is simple: If you are 62 or over, you
may buy the coupons, each good for a one-way trip within
the lower 48 states and sometimes beyond. On long flights,
they can save you a good deal of money. As an alternative,
almost every airline—both domestic and foreign—also
gives senior travelers and a traveling companion of any age
a 10 percent discount on most individual tickets. One airline even issues passes that allow seniors with wanderlust
virtually unlimited travel at a fixed rate from a home city
for a choice of four months or a year.

You get these nice offers because you, the mature population, have proved to be the hottest travel market around,

a vast and growing group of careful consumers with money in your pockets and time on your hands midweek and during the slack off-peak travel periods, just when the airlines are eager to fill up seats.

But, first, keep in mind:

■ Find a good travel agent and ask him or her to get you the *lowest possible fare*. Mention the fact that you qualify for a senior discount, but be prepared to jump ship if you can get a better deal by going with a special promotional rate or a supersaver fare—although sometimes your discount can cut these low fares even lower. Most airlines now offer promotional fares during off-peak seasons, sometimes specifically for seniors. Watch for these sales because they are usually the cheapest way to go, although in most cases you can't deduct the regular senior discount from them.

■ Keep in mind that the restrictions you must fly by may not be worth the savings. Always examine the fees and conditions and decide whether you can live with them. There may be blackout periods around major holidays when you can't use your privileges, departures only on certain days or hours, restrictions on the season of the year, or stiff penalties for flight changes. In some plans, you must travel the entire distance on one airline even if connections are poor. It's not always easy to sort out the offers.

■ Before you decide to buy Continental's four-month or yearly passport that lets you travel up to once a week, figure out how many trips you're likely to make during the next year. Unless you see clear savings, you are better off with individual tickets or coupon books. However, if you travel frequently, or would do so once you had the pass, then it could prove to be an excellent buy if you can live with the restrictions.

■ A 10 percent senior discount is obviously better than nothing, but on high-mileage trips you'll probably do much better with a coupon book if you fly often enough to use them up.

■ Try to couple your 10 percent senior discount with ultimate supersaver fares, which require 30-day advance purchase and include other restrictions.

■ Be prepared to present valid proof of age at the check-in counter. It's possible that your discount will not be honored if you don't have that proof with you, and you will have to pay the difference.

■ Virtually all airlines allow younger travel mates to fly with the same senior discount when you fly together for the entire trip.

■ Be flexible. To get the best fares when you use your senior discount, plan to fly at off-peak times, when the rest of the population isn't rushing off to faraway places. For example, noontime or late-night flights can be much cheaper than early-morning or dinnertime flights. Consider leaving on a different day—fares are often lower midweek or on Saturday. And obviously, flying off-season, when children aren't on vacation and there are no major holidays, may pay off with better prices.

■ Senior airline coupon books are one of the outstanding buys today, although their prices have been steadily rising. With coupons, a 62-plus traveler can go anywhere within the lower 48 states and sometimes beyond for much less than the regular coach fares for long trips, and often substantially less than even the best sale fares around. Each coupon is good for a one-way trip, including connecting flights if required. Two coupons are generally required each way for Alaska and Hawaii.

■ The coupons have many additional advantages. For example, unlike other low-fare tickets that require round-trip reservations, those you get with your coupons allow you to fly one way and decide later when you will return. You don't have to stay over a Saturday night and, in most cases, you must make your reservations only 14 days before departure. You may use them, too, for instant travel on a standby basis, infinitely cheaper than the usual last-minute fares. With some exceptions, coupons for younger companions are not available, but you will get frequent flyer mileage for the miles you fly. On US Airways, seniors may also use their coupons for children under 12 who accompany them.

■ Eight-coupon books, now issued by only a couple of airlines, cost less per flight than four-coupon books. After you've used the first coupon in your book, the remaining vouchers become nonrefundable, so don't buy the books unless you are sure you will use them all. Once issued, the coupons must be redeemed for tickets and reservations made within a year, but in most cases you have another year to travel because you can book flights 12 months ahead. You may buy the booklets from your travel agent or the airline.

■ Remember that it costs the same for a few hundred miles as for several thousand, so don't waste your coupons on short trips. In other words, the longer the distance, the greater the savings. For shorter trips, you are probably better off with the 10 percent senior discount.

■ Book your flights as early as possible for the best fares and the most available seats. Seats for travel on senior coupons or senior discounts are limited and may not be issued on some flights.

■ If you want to join a private airline VIP club so you can spend extra time at airports in peace and comfort, complete with snacks and free drinks, copy machines, private telephones, luggage storage areas, and sometimes even showers, remember that you can buy a lifetime membership at age 60 or 62 for about half the regular fee from most major airlines. Your younger spouse also gets a senior discount.

Now for some of the good deals awaiting you. Be advised that airfares and airline policies can change overnight—and often do—so always call the airline that interests you for an update.

U.S. AIRLINES
AIR SOUTH AIRLINES
Air South flies throughout the Southeast as well as to Chicago and New York. If you are going its way and are at least 55 years old, ask for the Senior Fare which will save you some money and earn you frequent flyer credits. It's yours

any day of the week when space is available. To get the Senior Fare, you must buy your tickets at least seven days in advance.

Before taking advantage of your age, however, ask whether there is a two-for-one sale going on, an even better deal if you are flying with a younger companion because your travel mate gets to go free.

For information: Call your travel agent or 800-247-7688.

ALASKA AIRLINES

Fly on Alaska Airlines at 62-plus and you'll get 10 percent off almost all fares along with frequent-flyer credits. So will a traveling companion of any age.

For information: Call your travel agent or 800-426-0333.

AMERICA WEST

America West's Senior Saver Pack, for travelers 62 and over, may be purchased in booklets of four coupons, each to be traded for a one-way ticket within a year. Priced below those of most other airlines, the coupons allow you to fly wherever the airline goes within the continental U.S. and Canada. However, travel days are limited. You may fly on coupon tickets only from Monday noon through Thursday noon and all day Saturday. And there are many blackout dates when you cannot use them. Flights to Anchorage require two coupons each way. Reservations must be made at least 14 days in advance, although standby is permitted.

America West also gives you and a younger companion a discount of 10 percent on the regular coach fares. But be sure to ask about the special senior fares offered on some flights—they may prove to be an even better buy.

For information: Call your travel agent or 800-235-9292.

AMERICAN AIRLINES

American Airlines has two good offers for passengers over 62. One is a 10 percent discount on any regular fare, even the lowest, for you and a traveling companion.

The other is its Senior TrAAveler Coupon Books, which give you four coupons per book. Traded in for a ticket, each coupon is good for travel one way in the continental U.S. as well as Puerto Rico and the U.S. Virgin Islands. Flights to Hawaii require two coupons each way.

You may travel any day of the week, but you must buy your tickets at least 14 days in advance of your flight or fly standby. There is no refund on the coupons and no change of itinerary on one-way tickets, although if you don't take your reserved flight, you may use the ticket for a standby seat. On round trips, you may change your outbound flight at least 14 days before the flight for a $50 service charge. You may change your return anytime for a $50 service charge. Seats are limited, but you will be entitled to frequent-flyer credits for all the miles you fly. The same privileges apply to flights on American Eagle, AA's commuter airline affiliate.

Another program, Senior SAAvers Club, is no longer open for enrollment, but if you are already a lifetime member, you'll continue to get its newsletter and a 10 percent discount on your fares.

For information: Call your travel agent or 800-433-7300 for reservations. For the Senior TrAAveler Coupon Books, call 800-237-7981.

CARNIVAL AIRLINES

This low-fare airline out of Florida gives passengers over 60 a discount of 10 percent off virtually all fares every day of the year.

It also offers over-60s its Senior Sampler Pack, four one-way flight coupons for travel between Florida and the Northeast. The coupon books are sold for a flat fee, guaranteeing the fare even during the high season. There are no minimum or maximum stays, penalties for changes, Saturday-night stays, or advance bookings required. The coupons must be traded within a year but they may also be used to travel standby if you want to take your chances on getting a seat at the last minute. Seats, of course, are limited and there are several blackout periods around major holidays throughout the year. Once ticketed, it will cost you $50 to change your reservation. You may collect mileage points for your flights when you use either the coupons or the senior discount.
For information: Call your travel agent or 800-824-7386.

CONTINENTAL AIRLINES

Continental Airlines offers some of the best deals around for senior travelers and now gives you a choice of three options. First, there's the 10 percent discount on all fares, even the lowest, for you and a younger companion if you are at least 62. Simply ask for it and be ready to prove your age. You'll get mileage points.

The next choice is Freedom Trips, booklets of four or

eight coupons, each to be traded for a one-way ticket on flights in the continental U.S., Canada, Mexico, the Caribbean, the U.S. Virgin islands, Puerto Rico, and Bermuda. Two coupons are required for flights to Hawaii and Alaska. You must make reservations at least 14 days in advance or travel standby. You may fly any day except during blackouts around major holidays and you are entitled to frequent flyer points for the miles you fly. You must redeem your coupons within a year after purchase, but you have another year to complete your travel.

Continental is the only U.S. airline that offers a senior pass, the third choice for people over 62. This is the Freedom Passport, a great bargain if you can't stand staying home for long and must be on the move. For a flat fee, it allows you a single one-way flight once a week. The Domestic Freedom Passport, available for either four months or one year, permits travel within mainland U.S., and to Puerto Rico, Montreal, and St. Thomas. Add-ons at a surcharge are yours for trips to Alaska, Hawaii, and foreign destinations. The Global Passport, more expensive, good for a year, covers travel in all 50 states plus Mexico, the Caribbean, Central America, and Europe.

A companion of any age may purchase any Passport at the same price. Travel is permitted between noon on Monday through noon on Thursday and all day Saturday and you must stay over a Sunday night. There are holiday blackouts and only a limited number of seats on each flight are made available for Passport holders. You are allowed a single one-way trip per week but will not earn mileage credits. You may travel to the same destination from your home city a maximum of three times.

For information: Call your travel agent or 800-525-0280 for reservations. For Freedom Passports or Freedom Trips, call 800-441-1135.

DELTA AIRLINES

At age 62, you have three options offered by Delta. The first is a 10 percent discount on virtually all published fares, even including most sale fares, for you and a travel partner for flights within the U.S. (including Alaska, Hawaii, San Juan and the U.S. Virgin Islands) as well as to and from Canada and Mexico. Seats are limited, so book early. Of course you'll be entitled to mileage points when you use the discount.

Your second option is the Young at Heart Coupon program that lets you purchase booklets of four coupons for a flat fee. The coupons must be traded within a year for tickets to any Delta city in the continental United States, Puerto Rico, the U.S. Virgin Islands, or Canada, with two coupons required for flights to Alaska or Hawaii. You may fly any day of the week and you'll get frequent flyer credits for your miles. Reservations or changes must be made at least 14 days before departure, but once ticketed, flight changes are free. Remember that only a limited number of seats are available for passengers using senior coupons, so plan ahead. Without reservations, you may travel standby any time.

Probably the best deal of all is Delta's new Seniors Select Savings Plus program, a club with limited enrollment that promises significant discounts on coach and first class fares to any of 240 destinations served by Delta and Delta Connection in the continental U.S., Hawaii, and Alaska. No

Saturday night or minimum stay is required, nor are round-trip reservations (with a $10 surcharge on a one-way ticket purchase), but tickets must be purchased at least 14 days in advance. Benefits also include savings on rental cars, vacation packages, and cruises.

To become a member, you must be at least 62, pay an annual membership fee of $40, and belong to Delta SkyMiles, the airline's frequent-flyer plan. You may also enroll up to three companion members (adults over 62 or grandchildren age 2 through 12). The fee is $65 for two members and $70 for up to four. You'll earn frequent-flyer credit, but you can't combine the senior fares with any other deal, such as the 10 percent senior discount.

For information: Call your travel agent or 800-221-1212. To enroll in Senior Select Savings Plus, call 800-325-3750.

DELTA SHUTTLE

For shuttle flights between New York and Washington, D.C., or Boston, you get the Senior Fare, currently half of the fare for other adults—that is, if you are 62 and can provide evidence of that fact a half hour before flight time. And you are eligible for frequent-flyer credits for your miles. With this fare, you must fly between 10:30 A.M. and 2:30 P.M. or 7:30 P.M. and 9:30 P.M. Monday through Friday or all day Saturday or Sunday. No reservations are required. Just show up at the gate.

A second option is the Senior Flightpack, four one-way tickets that must be used within a year on flights that leave in off-peak hours: 10:30 A.M. to 2:30 P.M. or 7:30 to 9:30 P.M. Monday through Friday and all day Saturday or Sunday. To be eligible for this good deal, you must be at least

62. Frequent-flyer credits apply. The Flightpack may be purchased only in a shuttle city—although you may buy a voucher through your travel agent and trade it for the booklet when you arrive at the airport.
For information: Call your travel agent or 800-221-1212.

HAWAIIAN AIRLINES

At age 60, you and a traveling companion are entitled to a 10 percent discount on some first-class and high-end coach fares on flights between the mainland and Hawaii. Ask about promotional fares before using the senior discount.
For information: Call your travel agent or 800-367-5320.

LONE STAR AIRLINES

This small regional carrier flies out of Dallas/Fort Worth to many small Midwest cities. If you are over 62, it will give you senior fares that are always less than the regular ones.
For information: Call your travel agent or 800-877-3932.

MIDWEST EXPRESS

Ten percent is the discount on published fares for people over the age of 62 on Midwest Express, an airline that flies out of Milwaukee to many cities in the U.S.
For information: Call your travel agent or 800-452-2022.

NORTHWEST AIRLINES

You and a companion, any age, get a senior discount of 10 percent, complete with frequent flyer credits, on most of Northwest's published fares when you've attained the age of 62.

At the same age, you're also eligible to purchase NorthBest Senior Coupons, a booklet of four coupons, each good for a one-way flight within the lower 48 states and Canada and to Puerto Rico. Two coupons are required each way to Hawaii and Alaska. For stopovers, an additional coupon is required. Reservations must be made 14 days in advance, but you may fly any time, any day, and collect mileage credits. Or you may fly standby any time. Coupons must be traded for tickets within a year.

For information: Call your travel agent or 800-225-2525.

RENO AIR

A low-cost carrier, Reno Air serves over a dozen cities in the Western U.S. and Canada, plus Chicago, and gives passengers over 62 a discount of 10 percent off all posted fares, with deeper discounts on some routes. No advance purchase is necessary.

For information: Call your travel agent or 800-736-6247.

SOUTHWEST AIRLINES

This airline, flying mainly in the southwestern United States, offers travelers over 65 special senior fares that vary from city to city and change frequently, but give you a discount of 10 to 30 percent off the lowest available fare on every flight every day. However, seats per flight are limited, so you can't always get them when you want them. Reservations are required but advance purchase is not necessary. You'll get mileage credits and the tickets are fully refundable.

If you are flying with a companion, maybe you'll want

to wait for one of Southwest's occasional Friends Fly Free sales. For passengers of all ages, it allows you to take a travelmate along for nothing. It may be cheaper than the senior fare.

For information: Call your travel agent or 800-435-9792.

TWA (TRANS WORLD AIRLINES)

TWA reduces the fare by 10 percent for travelers over 62 and companions of any age on almost all flights in the U.S. and Puerto Rico and some to Europe as well. Ask for the discount when you make reservations. You are entitled to frequent-flyer mileage.

The Senior Travel Pak is another alternative for travelers 62 or older. This gives you four or eight one-way domestic coupons at bargain prices (if you use them for long trips). Each coupon may be exchanged for a one-way ticket on flights in the mainland United States and Canada, plus Puerto Rico and Mexico City. Two coupons are required each way for trips to Hawaii. TWA's packets include discount certificates for a 20 percent reduction on a ticket to Europe, a $50 discount on a TWA Getaway Vacation package, and two upgrades on rental cars. You may travel any day of the week except the Wednesday before or the Sunday after Thanksgiving. Seats are limited so book yours early. Reservations must be made 14 days in advance, but you may travel standby anytime before your scheduled flight after you have traded your coupon for a ticket. You're entitled to mileage points.

TWA also issues companion four-coupon books, at a $100 surcharge, to be used when you and a younger travelmate fly together. All of the coupons must be used by the same person. The discount certificate for travel to Europe is included.

For information: Call your travel agent or 800-221-2000.

UNITED AIRLINES

United has three programs that benefit mature travelers. The first is a 10 percent discount at age 62 on excursion fares for you and any traveling companion. The discount also applies to United Express, selected fares from regional carriers, and all fares on the Shuttle by United.

Next good deal is the Silver TravelPac program for passengers over 62 which offers packets of four coupons at a flat fee, each coupon good for a one-way ticket within mainland United States, and to San Juan or Canada. Two coupons are required each way to Hawaii or Alaska (except from Seattle). They may be used for flights any day of the week, although there are blackouts during holiday seasons, and you must trade them for tickets within a year of the purchase date. Reservations must be made at least 14 days in advance, but you may use the coupons to fly standby. You'll get mileage credits for the miles you fly. Remember, seats at discounted fares are always limited, so plan ahead.

The third offer for mature travelers from UAL is United Silver Wings Plus, a travel club for seniors. You may join at age 55 and become eligible for many benefits, such as discounts on hotels, cruises, rental cars, and travel packages. A lifetime membership costs $225, but your welcome gifts include three $50 certificates to use against future travel and one $100 certificate for travel to Europe, plus bonus miles. Sign up for two years at $75 and you will receive three $25 travel certificates to help pay for future trips and other credits. Members earn mileage credits and upgrades and receive a newsletter.

At age 62, you and a companion get the 10 percent senior discount on all published fares, even discount fares, on United Airlines, United Express, and the Shuttle by United; on selected routes with international partners; and on some fares from regional carriers such as Air Canada and Mount Cook Airlines of New Zealand.

For information: Call your travel agent or 800-241-6522. For United Silver Wings Plus: 214-760-0022. For the SilverTravelPac: 800-633-6563.

SHUTTLE BY UNITED

Connecting 12 West Coast cities, the Shuttle by United gives passengers over 62 a discount of 10 percent on all flights. Reservations are required.

For information: Call your travel agent or 800-SHUTTLE (800-748-8853).

US Airways

You at age 62 and a travel companion at any age can count on a 10 percent discount on any US Airways fare, except sale fares.

This airline also offers passengers over 62 its Golden Opportunities Coupon Books. You may buy, at a flat fee, a book of four one-way coupons, each to be traded within a year for a ticket to any destination within the continental United States, Canada, Mexico, the U.S. Virgin Islands, and Puerto Rico, including flights on its commuter lines. Reservations must be made at least 14 days in advance, or you may travel standby anytime once a ticket has been issued. You may fly any day of the week and get mileage credits for your flights.

On flights between cities within Florida, one coupon will entitle you to one round trip.

And here's a bonus. As many as two of your grand-children, ages 2 through 11, may fly on your coupons if they travel with you.

For information: Call your travel agent or 800-428-4322.

US AIRWAYS SHUTTLE

You may fly at approximately half price on this airline's hourly shuttle flights between New York and Boston or Washington, D.C., if you are 62 and are willing to travel at off-peak hours. You may fly Monday through Friday at the senior rate from 10:00 A.M. to 2:00 P.M., after 7:00 P.M., or any time Saturday or Sunday.

For information: Call your travel agent or 800-428-4322.

VIRGIN ATLANTIC AIRLINES

On all flights between the United States and London, Virgin Atlantic gives you and a younger companion a 10 percent discount on all regular fares as soon as you turn 60. Ask for the discount when you make your reservations. In addition, the airline occasionally offers special two-for-one Senior Savings fares, for you at 60 and a travelmate of any age to fly for half-price. So keep your eyes open.

For information: Call your travel agent or 800-862-8621.

GOOD DEALS ON CANADIAN AIRLINES

AIR CANADA

If you are over 60, you and any traveling companion are eligible for a 10 percent reduction on fares in both economy and business class, even including some special promotional sales, for flights in Canada and the U.S. And on trips between Canada and the U.K. and the Caribbean. You'll get mileage credits as well.

In addition, at age 62 you and a companion can get the same discount on joint Air Canada flights with Continental and United Airlines.

For information: Call your travel agent or 800-776-3000 in the U.S.

CANADIAN AIRLINES INTERNATIONAL

The Canadian Golden Discount gives you a 10 percent reduction on all round-trip fares on Canadian Airlines and all of its partners to destinations within Canada and the continental U.S., and on certain fares to Hawaii and London. You get frequent-flyer credits for your mileage, and there are no special restrictions on time, day, or season.

For information: Call your travel agent or 800-426-7000 in the U.S.; 800-665-1177 in Canada.

GREYHOUND AIR

This new Canadian airline flies between many cities on the West Coast and Ontario and prides itself on its low special fares. If you must fly full fare, however, you will get 10 percent off if you are over the age of 60. Greyhound Air plans itineraries combining air travel with land tours aboard its familiar Greyhound buses.

For information: Call your travel agent or 800-661-8747 or 403-265-9111.

GOOD DEALS ON FOREIGN AIRLINES

Again, always inquire about special senior discounts when you book a flight, even if you don't see them listed here. Airlines change their policies with very little notice. Your travel agent can provide current information. Remember, too, that seasonal promotional fares available to all travelers can often be much lower than the fare you can get with your senior discount, so do your homework before committing yourself.

AEROLINEAS ARGENTINAS

On this airline, there's an offer of a 10 percent discount for passengers over 60 on posted fares for flights originating in the United States to any of its South American destinations.

For information: Call your travel agent or 800-333-0276.

AEROLITORAL

A commuter airline operated by Aeromexico that flies from several cities in the U.S. Southwest to Mexico, Aerolitoral offers a 50 percent discount on its regular economy fares to passengers over 62.

For information: Call your travel agent or 800-237-7113.

AEROMEXICO

It's 10 percent off the regular first-class or tourist fares on all Aeromexico routes, domestic and international, if you are over 62. There are blackouts for these senior fares, however, during major holidays.

For information: Call your travel agent or 800-237-6639.

AIR FRANCE

A 10 percent discount is yours at age 62 on Air France flights between its major U.S. gateway cities and France. The discount also applies to a traveling companion who may be younger, and it is deducted from almost every fare, including the Concorde, except for special promotional sales.

For information: Call your travel agent or 800-237-2747.

AIR INTER EUROPE

The major domestic airline in France, Air Inter Europe gives travelers over the age of 60 some excellent reduced fares on its flights within the country and to several destinations outside. Usually amounting to 40 to 60 percent off the full one-way fare, the senior tickets are available on almost all flights. Simply show proof of age when you purchase your tickets. This airline also sells air passes, for passengers of any age, that can be even better deals if you plan to do a lot of flying within a short period of time. So do some comparison shopping before you buy.

For information: Call your travel agent or 800-237-2747.

AIR JAMAICA

If you fly off-peak, which generally means spring and fall, you can take advantage of Air Jamaica's hefty 20 percent discount offered to passengers over the age of 60. Fly in a peak period and you'll get a 10 percent discount. So will one younger companion who's traveling with you. You must travel, first class or economy, on Tuesdays, Wednesdays, or Thursdays between all gateway cities in the U.S. and Jamaica. In addition, the senior discount applies on Saturday flights departing from Miami and Ft. Lauderdale. There's a service charge of $25 for cancelling your trip after you are ticketed.

For information: Call your travel agent or 800-523-5585.

ALITALIA

When you fly on Alitalia to its European destinations or Egypt, you qualify for a 10 percent discount when you are 62, as does a younger traveling companion. When you travel on an advance-purchase fare via Alitalia from the U.S. to Israel, you will get a 15 percent discount if you are 60. So will your companion if he or she accompanies you and is at least 55.

On certain domestic flights within Italy, seniors over 65 are offered special discounted Terza Eta (Third Age) fares. Be sure to ask for them.

For information: Call your travel agent or 800-223-5730.

BRITISH AIRWAYS

The good deal from British Airways for travelers over 60 and a companion is a discount of 10 percent on all advance-purchase economy-class airfares on trips from all 21 gateway cities in the U.S. and the four gateways in Canada to the UK and Europe. Also there is no charge for cancelling or changing your flights if you make your changes before your initial departure. A tip: Ask about the new All Seasons

Apex Fare for which tickets must be purchased 90 days or more in advance of departure. It may save you more money than your senior discount.

For information: Call your travel agent or 800-247-9297.

EL AL

Travelers over the age of 60 and their spouses over 55 are entitled to El Al's senior fare, which gives you a discount of about 15 percent off the regular Apex fare between the U.S. and Israel. You may stay for up to two months, a 14-day advance purchase is required, and there is a $50 fee for changing your return flight.

But, before accepting this deal, check out the cheaper Superapex fare with its maximum stay of 45 days. It may work out better for you.

Traveling with your grandchildren? If they are under 12, the first one flies at 25 percent off, the second at 50 percent off, and the third at 75 percent off.

For information: Call your travel agent or 800-223-6700.

FINNAIR

On flights between New York and Helsinki, Finland, you will get a 10 percent reduction off the regular economy fares if you are 62 years old or more. Travel companions of any age get the same discount.

For information: Call your travel agent or 800-950-5000.

IBERIA

Iberia gives you 10 percent off regular published fares for transatlantic flights originating in North America, except on special sales. You must have reached 62 to get the privilege, but you may take a younger companion who pays the same fare.

For information: Call your travel agent or 800-772-4642.

KLM ROYAL DUTCH AIRLINES

KLM's discount for people over the age of 62 is 10 percent on all nonpromotional fares between the U.S. and its European destinations. A companion of any age is entitled to the same reduction in fare if you travel together for the entire journey.

For information: Call your travel agent or 800-374-7747.

LUFTHANSA

At age 60, you can get a 10 percent reduction on most fares, including first-class, business, and economy, for yourself and another adult travel mate, on Lufthansa flights to and from the U.S. and Germany. Seats are limited and you must request the discount when you make your reservations.

For information: Call your travel agent or 800-645-3880.

MARTINAIR HOLLAND

Billing itself as "The Other Dutch Airline," Martinair Holland flies from nine North American gateway cities to Amsterdam and beyond, and offers its lowest economy fares to travelers who are at least 60 (and younger companions) and waives the usual restrictions. In other words, no advance purchase is required, fares have an "open" return policy, and tickets are valid for travel from seven to 365 days. Seniors, as well as others, may choose instead to fly standby and pay even less.

For information: Call your travel agent or 800-MARTI-NAIR (800-627-8462).

MEXICANA AIRLINES

A senior discount of 10 percent applies to most Mexicana international flights between gateway cities in the U.S. or Canada and Mexico, except for a blackout period around major holidays. You must be 62, but your traveling companion may be younger and get the same rate.
For information: Call your travel agent or 800-531-7921.

SABENA (BELGIAN WORLD AIRLINES)

At 62, you are entitled to a 10 percent discount on all fares (including nonrefundable fares) from the United States to Belgium and via Brussels to other Sabena destinations in Europe. In addition, Sabena offers special senior fares to travelers over 60 and spouses over 55 on round-trip flights to Israel. You must stay a minimum of six days and a maximum of two months (for an added fee, you may stay up to six months) and book a week in advance. Bonus: one free stopover in the United States and another in Europe on your way to or from Tel Aviv.
For information: Call your travel agent or 800-955-2000.

SAS (SCANDINAVIAN AIRLINES SYSTEM)

Flying on SAS across the Atlantic Ocean to Scandinavia and elsewhere from U.S. gateway cities, you'll get a 10 percent reduction on most fares if you are 62 or older. Within Denmark, you are also entitled to a senior discount that varies according to the route, but for this you must wait until you are 65. Remember to take your passport with you for proof of age when you purchase your tickets.

For information: Call your travel agent or 800-221-2350.

SWISSAIR

Swissair offers two good options to travelers over the age of 62 (in Canada, that's 60) and their younger traveling companions. One is a 10 percent discount on almost all published fares on flights from its eight U.S. and Canadian gateway cities to destinations in Europe. Yours for the asking, it is available on flights all year round and every day of the week.

The second deal from this airline is a 10 percent discount for you and a companion, up to $100 per person, when you book a Swissair land package.

For information: Call your travel agent or 800-221-4750. For the land program, call Swisspak, 800-688-7947.

TAP AIR PORTUGAL

Your discount from this airline if you are at least 62 is 10 percent off almost any fare on flights between the United States and Portugal, Madeira, and the Azores. The discount applies to a younger flying partner as well. Be prepared to present your passport or driver's license as proof of age. You may fly anytime.

For information: Call your travel agent or 800-221-7370.

8

Beating the Costs of Car Rentals

Never rent a car without getting a discount or a special promotional rate. Almost all car-rental agencies in the United States and Canada give them to all manner of customers, including those who belong to over-50 organizations (see Chapter 19) or have reached a certain birthday. The discount that's coming to you as a senior member of society can save you some money although promotional sales may save you more. Refer to the membership material sent by the group to which you belong for information about your discount privileges.

But, first, keep in mind:

■ Car-rental agents may not always volunteer information about senior discounts or special sales, so always ask for it when you reserve your car.

■ Don't settle for a senior discount or senior rate too hastily without investigating the possibility of an even better deal. Shop around yourself or ask your travel agent to find the *lowest available rate or package* at the time you are going to travel, and don't forget to ask about airport fees, taxes, and other extra charges. Senior discounts are usually given on the full published rental rate. So special promotional rates—in other words, sales—or even weekend rates are almost always better, sometimes much better. On the other hand, if you can get the senior discount *on top of the lowest posted rate*, regular or promotional, that's the deal you want. Thrifty, for example, guarantees a 10 percent discount off the lowest available rate.

■ When you reserve a car, always ask for a confirmation number. When you pick up your car, remember to verify the discount and ask if a better rate has become available since you booked.

■ When you call to ask about rates or reservations, always be armed with your organization's ID number and your own membership card for reference.

■ Special savings may not be available at every location, so you need to remember to check them out every time you make a reservation.

■ If you want to rent a car in Europe, be sure to ask the rental agency if it imposes age restrictions on drivers. These vary by country and agency. One agency, for example, denies rentals to people over 65 in Greece and Northern Ireland, or over 75 in Ireland and Israel. In the United Kingdom and Ireland, most agencies will not rent a car to a driver over 75. So make your age clear when you make your reservation. Shop around, and also consider leasing a car, in which case age may not be an issue.

ADVANTAGE RENT-A-CAR

Concentrated in the southwestern states, Advantage gives a 5 percent discount to members of AARP when they use the toll-free number below.

For information: Call your travel agent or 800-777-5500.

ALAMO RENT A CAR

The Senior Citizen Discount for anyone over the age of 50 takes 10 percent off the lowest available retail rate for weekly rentals and 3 percent off daily rentals of compact cars and up. A 24-hour advance reservation is required and so is a request for the senior discount.

For information: Call your travel agent or 800-GO-ALAMO (800-462-5266).

AVIS RENT-A-CAR

Special rates amounting to 5 to 20 percent, sometimes more, off the rates are given to members of AARP, CARP, and Mature Outlook.

For information: Call your travel agent or 800-331-1800.

BUDGET RENT-A-CAR

If you are 50 years old and have an AARP or CARP card, you'll get 5 percent taken off Budget's standard car rental rates (except for economy-size cars) in the U.S. Better yet, in Florida this agency will give you 10 percent off all rates (except for economy-size cars) if you are 50. In Canada, CARP and AARP members get special senior rates.

For information: Call your travel agent or 800-527-0700.

DOLLAR RENT A CAR

Small discounts that vary by location are offered to members of AARP.

For information: Call your travel agent or 800-800-4000.

ENTERPRISE CAR RENTALS

AARP members are entitled to 10 percent off the regular rental rates for compact or larger cars at Enterprise.

For information: Call your travel agent or 800-325-8007.

HERTZ CAR RENTAL

If you are a member of AARP, Mature Outlook, Y.E.S., or the National Association of Retired Federal Employees, you are entitled to savings, usually from 5 to 15 percent, on Hertz rental cars.

For information: Call your travel agent or 800-654-3131.

KEMWEL CAR RENTAL

A major car-rental operator in Europe, Kemwel now has locations in many cities throughout the United States, most of them currently in California, Florida, and Texas. To be eligible for a 5 percent discount on the regular rates, you must be 65 or older.

For information: Call your travel agent or 800-678-0678.

NATIONAL CAR RENTAL

With this rent-a-car agency, you get a minimum 10 percent discount on all rentals except on most sale rates, if you are a member of AARP, CARP, or Mature Outlook.

For information: Call your travel agent or 800-227-7368.

PAYLESS CAR RENTAL

Mature travelers—50 and over—get a straightforward 5 percent discount off any rate any time when they've joined the Nifty 50 Plus program. It's free. Join at any location or by calling the number below.

For information: Call your travel agent or 800-PAYLESS (800-729-5377).

THRIFTY RENT-A-CAR

Now here's a really good deal: If you are 55 or more, Thrifty guarantees you a 10 percent discount off its lowest available rates, *including* promotional sale rates, at all of its locations in the U.S. and Canada. So shop for the best price, then add your senior discount before you make your reservation.

For information: Call your travel agent or 800-367-2277.

VALUE RENT-A-CAR

Just show your AARP card and you will get a 5 percent discount on the regular rates for compact or larger cars.

For information: Call your travel agent or 800-468-2583.

9

Saving a Bundle on Trains, Buses, and Boats in North America

Getting around town, especially in a city where driving is not a practical option, probably means depending on public transportation to get you from hither to yon. Remember that, once you reach a particular birthday—in most cases, your 60th or 65th—you can take advantage of some good senior markdowns on trains, buses, and subways (unfortunately, taxis have yet to join the movement). All you need is a Medicare card, a Senior ID card, or your driver's license to play this game, which usually reduces fares by half. Although you may find it uncomfortable at first to pull out that card and flash it at the bus driver or ticket agent, it soon becomes easy. Do it and you'll realize some nice savings.

And don't fail to take advantage of the bargains available to seniors on long-distance rail, bus, and boat travel as well.

RIDING THE RAILS

Probably every commuter railroad in the United States and Canada gives older riders a break, although you may have to do your traveling during off-peak periods when the trains are not filled with go-getters rushing to and from their offices. Ask for your discount when you purchase your ticket.

As for serious long-distance travel, many mature travelers are addicted to the railroads, finding riding the rails a leisurely, relaxed, romantic, comfortable, economical, and satisfying way to make miles while enjoying the scenery.

So many passes and discounts on railroads are available to travelers heading for other parts of the country that sorting them out becomes confusing. But, once you do, they will help stretch your dollars while covering a lot of ground.

See the country-by-country section in Chapter 4 for the best deals on trains in foreign countries for travelers of a certain age.

AMTRAK

To accommodate senior travelers, Amtrak offers a 15 percent discount on the lowest available coach fares, including All-Aboard America Passes, and on some Canadian routes, every day of the week to anyone over 62. It is also available on the Metroliner Service on Saturdays and Sundays but does not apply to the Auto Train or sleeping accommodations. Consider taking your grandchildren with you because, up to age 15, they ride at 50 percent of the regular adult fare. Also keep your eyes open: Amtrak sometimes offers senior specials.

The lowest coach fares often sell out quickly, so try to

book early. Not all fares are available on every train and some have restrictions that may not suit your plans, which means you should always ask questions before you buy. *For information:* Call Amtrak at 800-USA-RAIL (800-872-7245).

ALASKA RAILROAD

Passengers over 65 are entitled to a 25 percent reduction in weekend fares during the winter months—late September through mid-May—on the Aurora Train running between Anchorage and Fairbanks.
For information: Call Alaska Railroad at 800-544-0552.

VIA RAIL CANADA

The government-owned Canadian passenger railroad offers you, at age 60, 10 percent off the regular coach fare every day of the year with no restrictions. Add this 10 percent to the 40 percent reduction on off-peak travel, available to all ages and applicable any day of the week except Friday and Sunday, and you end up with tickets that are half price. Tickets at the off-peak rate must be purchased at least five or seven days in advance. However, the number of seats sold at this rate is limited, so plan ahead and buy your tickets as early as possible.

When you reach the age of 60, you are also eligible to buy a Canrailpass at a 10 percent discount. The pass allows you to travel for any 12 days during a 30-day period anywhere on Via Rail's transcontinental system. You may board and deboard the train as many times as you wish, stopping wherever you like along the way.
For information: Via Rail Canada, PO Box 8116, Station

A, Montreal, Quebec H3C 3N3. For reservations or a Can-railpass, call your travel agent.

GOING BY BUS

Never, never board a bus without showing the driver your Senior ID card, because even the smallest bus lines in the tiniest communities (and the largest—New York City, for example) in this country and abroad give senior discounts, usually half fare. In Europe, your senior rail pass is often valid on major motorcoach lines as well, so always be sure to ask.

GREYHOUND BUS LINES

When Greyhound does the driving, you are entitled to a 10 percent reduction on any last-minute "walk up" fares if you have passed your 55th birthday. Be prepared to show a photo ID with proof of age. It pays to plan ahead, however, because advance-purchase fares are usually a much better deal than what you'll get with your senior discount, and sometimes there are special sales that are even better than those. By the way, seniors over 55 also get a 10 percent discount on Greyhound's Ameripass, which gives you unlimited travel for 7, 15, or 30 days to any U.S. destinations.

For information: Call your local Greyhound reservation office or 800-231-2222.

GREYHOUND LINES OF CANADA

Here you'll get 10 percent off all regular fares, any day of the week, all year around, if you are a traveler over the age of 60 with a valid ID. What's more, if you're accompanied by a younger companion and buy your tickets seven days in advance, the companion travels for half the senior fare. A good deal all around.

For information: Call Greyhound Canada, 800-661-8747 or 403-265-9111.

GRAY LINE TOURS

Gray Line is an association of many small independent motorcoach lines throughout the country, all of which offer sight-seeing and package tours. Most, but not all, of them give a 15 percent discount on sight-seeing tours to members of AARP at age 50 and sometimes other seniors as well. Find out if you qualify before buying your ticket.

For information: Call your travel agent or the Gray Line Tours office in your area.

ONTARIO NORTHLAND

This passenger railroad serving northeastern Ontario gives travelers over the age of 60 a 25 percent fare reduction any day of the year. Sometimes you can get this discount in addition to others offered in the off-season.

For information: Ontario Northland, 65 Front St. West, Toronto, ON M5J 1E6; 800-268-9281 or 416-314-3750.

TRENTWAY WAGAR

A bus line that services southwest Ontario and the Niagara Peninsula, this company offers discounts ranging from 10 to 25 percent to passengers over the age of 60.

For information: Trentway Wagar, 791 Webber Ave., Peterborough ON K9J 7A5; 800-461-7661 or 705-748-6411.

VOYAGEUR COLONIAL LTD.

This Canadian motorcoach line's Club 60 offers you a discount of 25 percent on all regular one-way bus fares throughout the provinces of Quebec and Ontario, without prior reservations, seven days a week. Simply present proof of your age when you buy your tickets. You will also get discounts of varying amounts on Voyageur's one-day bus or riverboat tours out of such major cities as Montreal, Ottawa, and Kingston. But hold on: before you make a decision, check out the special excursion fares which may be even better.

A deal that may profit you even more than all of the above, however, if you plan extensive travel in these provinces is the Rout-Pass that is available to all ages and may be used for 15 consecutive days from mid-April through mid-November.

For information: Voyageur Colonial Ltd.; 514-842-2281 in Montreal; 613-238-5900 in Ottawa.

GOING BY BOAT
ALASKA MARINE HIGHWAY

Traveling on the Alaska Marine Highway during fall the off-season months is a bargain for foot passengers 65 and older. Between October and April, you sail for half the regular adult fare within Alaskan waters. The discount does not apply to vehicle or cabin space. Sometimes in the summer, too, there are half fares for seniors on several of the smaller vessels. The message is: always ask if a senior rate is available.

For information: Call 800-642-0066.

TOURING BY BOAT, RAIL, BUS
THE ALASKAPASS

With an AlaskaPass, you may travel on many kinds of surface transportation in Alaska and the Yukon Territory for a specified number of days, using gateways in British Columbia and the state of Washington. One set discounted price allows unlimited travel on participating ferries, buses, and trains. These include the Alaska Marine Highway ferries, the Alaskan Express Motorcoaches, the Alaska Railroad, Alaska Direct Bus Line, B.C. Rail, B.C. Ferries, Island Coach Lines, Greyhound Lines of Canada, and Norline Coaches (Yukon). You plan your own itinerary, make your own reservations, and pay for your transportation with the pass, using, if you like, suggested itineraries. If you are planning a trip, you may wish to send for the *AlaskaPass Handbook* ($5), which provides itineraries, lodging information, schedules, and general information for independent travelers.

The off-season—September 15 through May 15—is when all travelers, especially seniors, get a good deal on the cost of the pass. Then, an AlaskaPass Travelpass costs those over 65 $100 less than the discounted off-peak adult fare. *For information:* Call your travel agent or AlaskaPass at 800-248-7598. For the AlaskaPass Handbook, send $5 to AlaskaPass, PO Box 350, Vashon, WA, 98070.

10

Hotels and Motels: Get Your Over-50 Markdowns

Across the United States and Canada and throughout the rest of the world, major chains of hotels and motels (and individual establishments as well) are chasing the mature market—that's you. As a candidate for an increasing barrage of bargains in lodgings, you may not have to sell the family jewels to afford your next trip.

You don't even have to wait until you're eligible for Social Security to cash in on your maturity because most hotels, inns, and motels today offer discounts to you at age 50, usually requiring only proof of age or a membership card in a qualifying organization such as AARP. When you join a senior organization, you receive a list of the lodging chains that offer special rates to reward you for having lived so long and traveled so much. Other hotel chains give good discounts, sometimes as much as 50 percent off, to members of their own senior clubs that cost little or nothing to join and usually allow you to sign up at the front desk when you arrive at the hotel.

What all this means is that you should *never* make a hotel/motel reservation without making sure you are getting your senior privileges or an even better deal. Always ask for the senior discount, whether or not one is posted or mentioned in the hotel's literature. And *then* ask if that's the *best* rate you can get.

But, first, keep in mind:

If you want to take advantage of the privileges coming to you because of your age, be sure to do some advance research and planning with your travel agent or on your own.

- In this rapidly changing world, rates and policies can be altered in a flash, so an update is always advisable.
- Information about discounts is seldom volunteered. In most cases, you must arrange for discounts when you make your reservations and remind the desk clerk of them again when you check in. Do not wait until you're settling your bill because then it may be too late.
- Usually, over-50 discounts are subject to "space availability." That means it may be pretty hard to get them when you want to travel. So always book early, demanding your discount privileges, and try to be flexible on your dates in order to take advantage of them. Your best bets for space are usually weekends in large cities, weekdays at resorts, and non–holiday seasons.
- It's quite possible that a special promotional rate, especially in off-peak seasons or on weekends, may save you more money than your senior discount. Many hotels, par-

ticularly in big cities and warm climates, cut their prices drastically in the summer, for example. Others that cater mostly to business people during the week try to encourage weekend traffic by offering bargain rates if you stay over a Saturday night. Resorts are often eager to fill their rooms on weekdays. So always investigate all the possibilities before you get too enthusiastic about using your hard-earned senior discount, and remember to ask for the *lowest available rate.*

■ There are several chains of no-frills budget motels that may not offer discounts or too much in the way of amenities but do charge very low room rates and tend to be located along the most-traveled routes.

■ In some cases, not every hotel or inn in a chain will offer the discount. Those that do are called "participating" hotels/motels. Make sure the one you are planning to visit is participating in the senior plan.

■ In addition to the chains, many independent hotels and inns are eager for your business and offer special reduced rates. Always *ask* before making a reservation. Your travel agent should be able to help you with this.

■ Some hotel restaurants will give you a discount too, sometimes whether or not you are a registered guest.

■ By the way, your discount will not be given on top of other special discounts. One discount is all you get.

AMERISUITES

These all-suite accommodations designed for extended stays offer members of AARP a 10 percent discount off the regular rates.

For information: Call 800-982-6374.

ASTON HOTELS & RESORTS

Aston's Sun Club gives travelers 50 and older—and their roommates—up to 25 percent off room rates at its hotels and condominium resorts on Hawaii's four major islands, plus 10 percent off the daily rate or 20 percent off the weekly rate for a car rental. Ask for the special rates when you make your reservations and pick up a coupon book of discounts when you check in. Sun Club rooms are limited, so reserve early.

For information: Call 800-922-7866.

BEST INNS

At these inexpensive inns mainly in the Midwest and South, anyone over 50 gets $5 discounts weekdays, $10 Sunday nights.

For information: Call 800-237-8466.

BEST WESTERN INTERNATIONAL

Just prove that you're over 55 or show your AARP or CARP membership card, and you will get a 10 percent savings on all room rates every day of the year at every Best Western in the world. You will also be entitled to at least two special amenities at each hotel. These may include a complimentary continental breakfast, free local phone calls, a free newspaper, a room upgrade, late check-out, or other local offerings that may change by the season.

For information: Call 800-528-1234. For more details about the Mature Benefits program, call 800-603-2277.

BUDGET HOST INNS

A network of about 200 affiliated, mostly family-owned economy inns in 41 states and Canada, most Budget Host

Inns offer discounts to seniors that vary by location. They may be confirmed when you make your reservation or check in. When you call the toll-free reservation number, you will be transferred directly to the front desk of the inn in which you want to stay so you may ask as many questions as you like about such matters as the accommodations, facilities, rates, discounts, and directions to the property. *For information:* Call 800-283-4678.

BUDGETEL INNS

At these inexpensive motels located mainly in the South and Midwest, you will get a 10 percent discount just for being over 55. You will get it at 50 if you are a member of AARP. *For information:* Call 800-428-3438.

CALINDA HOTELS

See Choice Hotels.

AMERICAN EXPRESS SENIOR MEMBERSHIP

The first charge card developed especially for retirees, the Senior Member Card from American Express offers a special program of benefits and services. Senior Membership gives you the usual American Express charge privileges and customer services, plus some savings on travel, shopping, and dining; a special rate on SeniorNet membership; a quarterly newsletter; a free 24-hour hotline for medical and legal referrals or for sending urgent messages back home; a free 24-hour hotline to licensed pharmacists for questions about medications; and a reduced annual membership fee of $35 ($55 for the Gold Senior Member Card), if you are over 62. *For information:* Call 800-282-1700.

CAMBERLEY HOTELS

All six of these charming upscale hotels, some of them members of Historic Hotels of America, give AARP members 10 to 20 percent off the standard room rates.

For information: Call 800-555-8000.

CANADIAN PACIFIC HOTELS & RESORTS

These grand hotels and resorts throughout Canada give a 30 percent discount on regular room rates, subject to availability, to card-carrying members of AARP, CARP, and anybody else over 65.

Also, be sure to check out the special off-peak packages designed for older travelers at many Canadian Pacific hotels. For example: the Seniors Spring Fling, the Seniors Fall Getaway, the Sixty-Something room rate, and the Second Honeymoon.

For information: Call 800-441-1414.

CASTLE RESORTS & HOTELS
HAWAIIAN PACIFIC RESORTS

With a collection of 21 budget, moderate, and deluxe hotels and resort condominiums on all five Hawaiian islands, the Castle Group offers you a really good deal if you are at least 50 years old. It is a discount of up to 25 percent on the regular room rates, plus an air-conditioned subcompact car with unlimited mileage for an extra $20 a day.

For information: Call 800-367-5004.

CHOICE HOTELS

Choice Hotels is an international group of more than 2,800 inns in 38 countries with brand names that include Clarion, Comfort, Quality, Sleep, Econo Lodge, MainStay,

Calinda, and Rodeway. All of its properties in the U.S. and Canada take catering to older travelers very seriously and offer their Senior Saver Discounts to anyone over the age of 50. This means you will get 15 to 30 percent taken off the regular room rate when you make an advance reservation. Without a reservation, your discount is 10 percent. Because only a limited number of rooms are set aside for this program, it pays to plan ahead.

For information: Call your travel agent or 800-221-2222.

CLARION HOTELS & RESORTS

See Choice Hotels.

COLONY HOTELS & RESORTS

Over 40 participating midscale Colony condos and resorts throughout the United States, Hawaii, the Caribbean, Mexico, and a few other countries, give a 25 percent discount every day to AARP members. Non-cardholders who are over 55 are offered a 20 percent discount. Advance reservations are a must.

For information: Call 800-777-1700.

COMFORT INNS

See Choice Hotels.

CONRAD INTERNATIONAL HOTELS

The international subsidiary of Hilton USA, many Conrad Hotels in Europe, Australia, Mexico, Hong Kong, and the Caribbean participate in Hilton's Senior HHonors Program for over-60s. Members of the club are entitled to 25 to 50 percent off room rates. For more information, see Hilton Hotels.

COUNTRY HEARTH INNS

These economy motels in the South take 10 percent off the room rates for visitors over 50.

For information: Call 800-848-5767.

COUNTRY INNS & SUITES

These upper economy inns all over the world give you 10 percent off the regular rates if you are at least 55 years old, unless you belong to AARP or Mature Outlook, in which case you can get the discount at age 50.

For information: Call 800-456-4000.

COURTYARD BY MARRIOTT

Here AARP or CARP members are in luck—they get at least 10 percent off the regular room rates every day of the year. Most of these moderately priced hotels feature daily breakfast buffets, swimming pools, and exercise facilities. Advance reservations are recommended.

For information: Call 800-321-2211.

CROSS COUNTRY INNS

If you check in at one of these inns located in Ohio, Kentucky, or Michigan, you will get a 25 percent discount on your regular room rates every day of the year; but you must belong to AARP, have a Golden Buckeye card, or be over 60.

For information: Call 800-621-1429.

CROWNE PLAZA HOTELS & RESORTS

Here at participating locations you'll get a minimum of 10 percent off the regular room rates every day of the year

simply by showing your AARP membership card.
For information: Call 800-227-6963.

DAYS INNS

Join the September Days Club, the lodging industry's first senior travel club, and you'll be entitled to 10 to 50 percent discounts off the standard room rates at all 1,700 Days Inns worldwide. You'll also get a minimum of 10 percent reduction on meals at some locations, plus special rates on car rentals, travel and health insurance, and many trips and tours. A quarterly magazine keeps you up to date. Annual membership is $15 for you and your spouse.

If you aren't a member of the club, you'll still get a 10 percent discount on your room rate if you show a membership card from a senior organization such as AARP or CARP.

For information: Call 800-DAYS-INN (800-329-7466). In Canada, call 800-964-3434. To enroll in September Days Club, call 800-241-5050.

DOUBLETREE HOTELS

All Doubletree Hotels, Doubletree Club Hotels, and Doubletree Guest Suites now give members of AARP an offer that's hard to refuse—if you can make your travel plans early. With a membership card and a 21-day nonrefundable advance booking by credit card, you will pay only 40 to 50 percent of the regular room rates when there is space available. If you can't commit yourself so early, you will still be entitled to 10 percent off the room rates any time, any day, with no advance reservation. And individual Doubletree properties may also offer their own senior discounts that can reduce your cost even more, so be sure you're getting the best rate possible.

Hotel guests get something else, too: 10 percent taken off your bill for meals and nonalcoholic beverages at participating Doubletree restaurants.

For information: Call 800-222-8733.

DOWNTOWNER MOTOR INNS

See Red Carpet Inns.

DRURY INNS

These economy motels offer a 10 percent discount on the regular room rates at all of their 60 locations to anyone 50 or over. Just ask and have your proof of age handy.

For information: Call 800-325-8300.

ECONO LODGES

See Choice Hotels. Some rooms are specially designed for mature travelers.

ECONOMY INNS OF AMERICA

This economy lodging chain, with motels located near major highways in California, Florida, South Carolina, and Georgia, gives 10 percent off the room rates to AARP members and anyone over 55. Just ask for it.

For information: Call 800-826-0778.

EMBASSY SUITES

In some of its 125 upscale all-suite hotels, Embassy Suites gives a discount, usually about 10 percent, to travelers over

the age of 55. That means you'll have to make inquiries when you make your reservations. Amenities for guests include a complimentary cooked-to-order breakfast every morning and free beverages every evening.
For information: Call 800-362-2779.

FAIRFIELD INN BY MARRIOTT

At Marriott's economy lodging chain, you will get 10 percent deducted from your bill, complimentary continental breakfast, and free local calls if you belong to AARP or CARP, or are over 62.
For information: Call 800-228-2800.

FOUR POINTS HOTELS

See Sheraton Hotels & Resorts.

GRAND HERITAGE HOTELS

This group of upscale inns in the U.S., all restored "grande dame" hotels with historical significance, offers two good deals to guests over 55 or members of a recognized senior organization. The first is a discount of 20 percent off the regular rates any time. The alternative is 10 percent off any published package, promotional, or weekend room rate.
For information: Call 800-HERITAGE (800-437-4824).

HAMPTON INN HOTELS

The LifeStyle 50 program at this moderately priced group of more than 600 hotels entitles up to four guests to share a room at the one-person rate. All you have to do to get it is to show proof when you check in that one of you has had a 50th birthday.

For information: Call 800-HAMPTON (800-426-7866).

HARLEY HOTELS

Look for a 10 percent discount at 14 Harley properties in the Northeast simply by flashing your AARP or other senior organization card. On weekends, however, the weekend rate may be a better bet.

For information: Call 800-321-2323.

HAWAIIAN HOTELS & RESORTS

At 55, you'll get a 20 to 30 percent discount on the regular rates at any of these five hotels located on four Hawaiian islands, and sometimes other amenities such as free breakfast. At two of the hotels, special senior packages that are even better deals are also offered.

For information: Call 800-222-5642.

HAWAIIAN PACIFIC RESORTS

At 50, you are offered a discount on room rates up to 25 percent, plus a rental car for an extra $20 a day. See Castle Resorts & Hotels.

For information: Call 800-367-5004.

HILTON HOTELS WORLDWIDE

Hilton's Senior HHonors travel program is a very good deal for those over the age of 60 who do a lot of traveling. It gives you up to 50 percent off the regular rates at all participating Hilton Hotels in the U.S. and Canada as well as Hilton International and Conrad International Hotels all over the world. The annual membership fee for you and your spouse is $50; a lifetime membership currently costs $285.

As a member, you may reserve a second room at the same reduced rate for family or friends who are traveling with you and get late checkout privileges when possible. And you get 20 percent off the bill for dinner for two at participating hotel restaurants, whether or not you are guests of the hotel.

For those who don't join the Senior HHonors program but do belong to AARP, most Hiltons give a discount of 10 to 15 percent.

And, whatever your age, it's wise to sign up for Hilton HHonors Worldwide, a new guest reward program at Hiltons all over the world. It gives members both hotel points and airline frequent-flyer miles for each qualifying stay. It's free. Join by telephone or at the front desk of a participating hotel.

For information: Call 800-HILTONS (800-445-8667). To enroll in the Senior HHonors travel program, call 800-432-3600.

HOLIDAY INN WORLDWIDE

Holiday Inn Alumni, a travel club for mature travelers, is a good bet if you spend considerable time on the road because members receive a minimum of 20 percent off the regular room rates at more than 1,000 participating hotels worldwide. A continental breakfast for two comes with the room. The Club is advertised for people over 60, but you won't be turned away if you're only 50. As a member, you'll also have 10 percent deducted from your food bills at all meals in participating hotel restaurants in North America, whether you're a guest at the hotel or just dropping by for a meal. On your birthday, you'll get a complimentary dinner when another meal is purchased, again whether you're staying at the hotel or not. And, during the Thanksgiving and Christmas holidays, the club rates and benefits are extended to members of your family, too, but you must make the reservations yourself directly with the hotel you choose.

To join Holiday Inn Alumni, call the toll-free number below or sign up at a participating hotel. The first year is free. After that, the membership costs $10 a year, a fee that is waived if you stay a minimum of five nights a year at any Holiday Inn.

All is not lost, however, if you don't join the club because, with an AARP card, you will get a minimum of 10 percent discount at participating hotels.

For information: Call 800-HOLIDAY (800-465-4329) for reservations. To enroll in the club, call 800-ALUMNI-2 (800-258-6642).

HOWARD JOHNSON INTERNATIONAL

Here's what you'll get at Howard Johnson's scores of hotels, inns, or lodges in the U.S., Canada, and Mexico: a 20 percent discount off the regular rates if you are a member of AARP or CARP, or a 15 percent discount if you are a nonmember over the age of 60.

For information: Call 800-I-GO-HOJO (800-464-4656).

HYATT HOTELS & RESORTS

These upscale hotels in the U.S., Canada, and the Caribbean give guests over 65 a discount of up to 25 percent off the standard room rates. Just ask for it when you make your reservations. As usual, the senior rate is not always available, especially during peak travel times, so plan ahead.
For information: Call 800-233-1234.

KIMPTON HOTELS

All of Kimpton's 14 hotels in cities on the West Coast, most of them in San Francisco, with others in Portland, Seattle, and Los Angeles, have something good to offer mature travelers. The senior packages at these small, moderately priced "boutique" hotels (each one different) give you discounts ranging up to a third off the regular room rates and often include breakfast and evening wine service. You must be a member of AARP or at least 55 in most cases to qualify as a senior.
For information: Call 800-546-2622 and ask for the sales department.

KNIGHTS INNS

This budget motel chain with about 175 locations mostly in the East gives a discount of 10 percent throughout the year to anyone over 50.
For information: Call 800-THE-KNIGHTS (800-843-5644).

LA QUINTA INNS

With about 240 locations in the U.S., these motor inns are inexpensive and become even more so when you ask for your 10 percent discount. You'll get it if you are a member of AARP or a similar organization or if you are 55 and can prove it.

For information: Call 800-531-5900.

LK INNS

A budget chain in the Midwest, LK takes 10 percent off for AARP members and anybody else over 55.

For information: Call 800-282-5711.

THE LUXURY COLLECTION

See Sheraton Hotels & Resorts.

MAINSTAY SUITES

See Choice Hotels.

MARC RESORTS

If you are 55, a 25 percent discount is yours, except during holiday weeks, at Marc Resorts' 13 locations on five Hawaiian islands.

For information: Call 800-535-0085.

MARRIOTT HOTELS, RESORTS & SUITES

Marriott's program for over-50s is among the best deals around if you are a member of AARP or CARP and can plan ahead. With a membership card and a 21-day nonrefundable advance booking, you will get at least 50 percent off the regular rates at almost 200 participating locations. You must pay in advance for the entire stay by check or credit card when you make your reservation.

For those who can't commit themselves three weeks

ahead, there is an automatic 10 percent discount on regular room rates every day of the year for AARP or CARP card carriers.

There is also a 20 percent discount on meals (except on specials and alcoholic beverages) at most of the hotels and resorts for your party of up to eight people. This may be used as often as you like, and you are not required to be an overnight guest to get this discount, but you must belong to AARP or CARP or prove you're over 50. Always ask first if the hotel or resort is participating in the discount plan.

And more: you'll get a 10 percent discount on gift-shop purchases at participating hotels and resorts, except for certain items such as tobacco and candy.

Two hitches: the room discounts may not be available at all times, especially during peak periods, and some Marriotts do not participate in the seniors program.

For information: Call 800-228-9290.

MASTER HOSTS INNS & RESORTS

See Red Carpet Inns.

MOTEL 6

You can take advantage of a 10 percent discount on the room rates at these economy motels in more than 755 locations throughout the U.S. if you have an AARP card.

For information: Call 800-440-6000.

NOVOTEL HOTELS

Each of Novotel's nine midscale hotels in North America has its own senior program, but all of them offer good discounts to people of a certain age. The discounts are usually from 45 to 55 percent off the posted room rates, and the age at which they are offered varies from 55 to 65, so you will have to ask questions when you make your reservations. For example, at this writing Novotel New York takes 50 percent off for guests over the age of 60 when space is available.

For information: Call 800-NOVOTEL (800-668-6835).

OMNI HOTELS

Almost every one of these upscale hotels—there are 40 in the U.S.—take 10 percent off the corporate or weekend room rates every day of the week for members of AARP. Cardholders also get a 15 percent discount on food and nonalcoholic beverage bills in participating restaurants, any time of day for registered hotel guests and before 7 P.M. for those who are dropping in for a meal. To get the special room rate, reserve ahead and request the discount. In the restaurants, present your AARP card before you place your order.

For information: Call THE-OMNI (800-843-6664).

OUTRIGGER HOTELS & RESORTS

If you are 50 or older, Outrigger will give you 20 percent off regular published rates at any of its hotels and resorts in Waikiki on Oahu, Maui, Kauai, and the Big Island of Hawaii. You'll have your choice of a suite, an economy kitchenette, or a fully furnished condominium. Not only that, but you also will have the option of a rental car at $25 a day.

For members of AARP or CARP, the room discount is even better—25 percent all year, whenever rooms are available. Proof of age and/or membership are required at check-in.

For information: Call 800-OUTRIGGER (800-688-7444).

PARK INN INTERNATIONAL

This chain of over 50 hotels throughout the U.S. gives a 15 percent Silver Citizen discount to members of AARP and other nationally recognized senior organizations as well as unaffiliated travelers over the age of 60.

For information: Call 800-437-PARK (800-437-7275).

PASSPORT INNS

See Red Carpet Inns.

QUALITY INNS

See Choice Hotels.

RADISSON HOTELS WORLDWIDE

At this group of more than 330 individually owned hotels, inns, suites, and resorts all over the world, you will get a senior rate—if you're over 50—that, depending on the location, gives you up to 30 percent off the regular rate. The discount is yours any day of the week if rooms are available. Not only that, you and your party will also get 15 percent off the food and beverage bills at all hotel restaurants, whether or not you are a hotel guest if you belong to AARP or United Silver Wings Plus.

For information: Call 800-333-3333.

RADISSON SAS HOTELS

The older you are, the cheaper your stay at all Radisson SAS hotels in Europe, Asia, and the Middle East. The offer is available seven days a week for a limited number of rooms, so book well in advance, specifically request your discount, and make a confirmed reservation. What you get—a really good deal—is a discount that corresponds to your age once you've reached 65. At 65, you'll get a 65 percent reduction on the standard room rate; at 75, a 75 percent discount; and at 100, you stay free. Traveling with somebody else? The size of the discount is determined by the age of the oldest person in your party. Breakfast is included.

For information: Call 800-221-2350.

RAMADA CANADA

These 35 hotels across Canada offer their Mature Traveller discount to visitors over the age of 60. The discount varies from 10 to 25 percent off the standard room rates, depending on the location.

For information: Call 800-854-7854.

RAMADA LIMITED, INNS, AND PLAZA HOTELS

Ramada's Best Years Club, open to anyone at age 60, gives you 25 percent discounts, plus 15 frequent-stayer points for every dollar spent during your stays at more than 750 participating Ramadas. You'll get 3,000 bonus points when you sign up for the club and your accumulated points may be redeemed for free airline tickets, lodging, and travel awards. Other benefits include discounts on travel and car rentals and a quarterly newsletter. Lifetime membership costs $15. To join, sign up at any hotel or call the number below.

Another choice at participating Ramadas is a 15 percent discount for the over-50 members of AARP or CARP.

For information: Call 800-228-2828. To enroll in the Best Years Club, call 800-766-2378.

RAMADA INTERNATIONAL HOTELS & RESORTS

At these midscale hotels and resorts, all of them in Europe, if you are 60 years old or belong to any recognized senior organization, you're entitled to the senior rate, a minimum of 25 percent off the regular room rates every day of the year. Ask for it when you make your reservations.

For information: Call 800-854-7854. In Canada, 800-854-7854.

RED CARPET INNS

Almost all of the 285 Red Carpet Inns, Master Hosts Inns & Resorts, Passport Inns, Downtowner Motor Inns, Scottish Inns, and Sundowner Inns in the United States and Canada give anyone over 50 a 10 percent discount on room rates year-round, except perhaps during special local events when rooms are scarce.

For information: Call 800-251-1962.

RED LION HOTELS & INNS

To over-50s who present AARP, CARP, or Mature Outlook cards, Red Lions and Thunderbirds—all in the western states—give their Prime Rate, which amounts to 20 percent

off the regular room rates. Book ahead, because there are occasional blackout periods. In addition, some of their restaurants give you, hotel guests or not, 10 percent off food chosen from the regular menu except on some holidays.
For information: Call 800-547-8010.

RED ROOF INNS

An economy lodging chain with over 235 locations in 33 states, Red Roof offers seniors its RediCard+60 Club. You may join it at 60, paying a lifetime fee of $10 plus $2 for a spouse, and thereafter get a 10 percent discount on room rates. You can sign up when you check in.
For information: Call 800-843-7663.

RENAISSANCE HOTELS & RESORTS

When you make reservations at any of the luxury Renaissance Hotels in the U.S., Mexico, and 22 other countries around the world, ask for the senior rate if you are over 60 or a member of a recognized senior organization. You'll get a minimum of 25 percent off the published room rate any day of the year. Make advance reservations because, as always, rooms at special rates are limited.
For information: Call 800-228-9898.

RESIDENCE INNS BY MARRIOTT

These extended-stay all-suite accommodations complete with kitchens offer members of AARP or CARP a 15 percent discount on regular rates every day of the year. Continental breakfast is included.
For information: Call 800-331-3131.

RODEWAY INNS

See Choice Hotels. And check out Rodeway's new "senior-friendly" rooms, which feature such amenities as bright lighting and big TV control buttons.

SANDMAN HOTELS & INNS

All situated in western Canada, these 20 inns take 20 to 25 percent off the regular room rate if you are 55 or over. Show proof of age at check-in or, better yet, call the number below and ask for a Club 55 Card. It's free.
For information: Call 800-726-3626.

SCOTTISH INNS

See Red Carpet Inns.

SHERATON HOTELS & RESORTS

All Sheratons around the world give you a break if you are over 60 or a member of AARP, CARP, or a long list of other recognized senior organizations, and are traveling for pleasure not business. That's a 25 percent discount off the published room rates. You may also reserve another room for family members at the senior rate when you are traveling together. Sometimes, however, these hotels have special sales going on that are better than the senior rate, so always ask for the best available price at the hotel you plan to visit. ITT Sheraton Corporation's other hotel groups, The Luxury Collection and Four Points Hotels, give seniors the same discount at all of their locations.

As for the seven resort hotels in Hawaii, these offer special senior packages that include the 25 percent discount

as well as other benefits such as airport transfers, room upgrades, breakfast, and rental-car discounts.
For information: Call 800-325-3535.

SHONEY'S INNS

Economy lodgings, Shoney's approximately 90 motels and inns scattered throughout the southeastern states take 15 percent off the room rates for members of AARP any time, any day of the week. If you are not a member but are at least 55 years old, you will get a 10 percent discount when rooms are available.
For information: Call 800-222-2222.

SLEEP INNS

See Choice Hotels.

SONESTA INTERNATIONAL HOTELS

This collection of hotels, some in exotic locations, gives members of AARP a 15 percent discount off the regular rates. You must make reservations in advance, of course. Also check out Sonesta's seasonal specials, usually in the fall, which may prove to be even better deals.
For information: Call 800-SONESTA (800-766-3782).

SUMMERFIELD SUITES

If you stay in one of these suites and you belong to AARP, be sure to ask for your 10 percent discount.
For information: Call 800-833-4353.

SUNDOWNER INNS

See Red Carpet Inns.

SUPER 8 MOTELS

Almost all of these over 1,400 no-frills economy motels in the U.S. and Canada give a 10 percent discount to members of over-50 clubs or people over a certain age, that age differing according to the location. Some locations offer discounts up to 50 percent on occasion, so be sure to make inquiries before booking a room.

For information: Call 800-800-8000.

DISNEY DISCOUNTS

If you plan frequent visits to Walt Disney World in Florida or Disneyland in California, think about acquiring a Magic Kingdom Club Gold Card. For visitors 55 and over, it provides a two-year membership for $50 ($15 less than the regular membership price), entitling you to reduced ticket prices to Disney theme parks worldwide, 10 to 30 percent off at some Disney resort hotels, and 10 to 15 percent discounts on select Disney restaurants.

For information: Call 800-56-DISNEY (800-563-4763).

SUSSE CHALETS

At most of these motels and inns scattered from Maine to Maryland, you will get a 10 percent discount at age 60 if you ask for it.

For information: Call 800-5-CHALET (800-524-2538).

THRIFTLODGES

See Travelodge.

THUNDERBIRD MOTOR INNS

See Red Lion Hotels & Inns.

TRAVELODGES AND THRIFTLODGES

All Travelodge and Thriftlodges, more than 500 of them throughout North and South America, have a nice straightforward plan for older travelers. This is a simple unrestricted 15 percent discount off the room rates any time, any night, for any persons over the age of 50. No advance reservations are required and there are no blackout periods, although the discount is, as everywhere, subject to the availability of rooms.

Travelodge also offers its free instant-enrollment Classic Travel Club for over-50s which gives you the 15 percent discount every day, plus some additional benefits, among them a discount on rental cars and express check-in. Sign up at the front desk or by calling the number below.

For information: Call 800-578-7878. For details about the Classic Travel Club, call 800-526-CLUB (800-526-2582).

VAGABOND INNS

Vagabond's Smart Senior Program is one of the better deals around. It gives you 30 percent off the standard rates at age 55 at all (except one) of these economy inns on the West Coast with or without a reservation. This group of hotels also has its Vagabuck Program which gives you $5 in play money every time you check out. Use it the next time you stay at a Vagabond Inn.

For information: Call 800-522-1555.

VILLAGER LODGES

At most of these economy extended-stay motels, you can get a room with a kitchenette at a discount of 10 percent off the daily rate if you belong to AARP or are over the age of 60.

For information: Call 800-328-7829.

WELLESLEY INNS

This group of "luxury budget inns" located on the East Coast, mostly in Florida, gives members of AARP a discount of 10 percent off the regular room rates. Make sure, however, that the senior rate gives you the best deal—sometimes these inns run specials that are even better. Complimentary continental breakfast is included.

For information: Call 800-444-8888.

WESTCOAST HOTELS

If you are 55 or over, you are offered discounts ranging from 10 to 44 percent off the regular rates at this group of moderately priced hotels in the West.

For information: Call 800-426-0670.

WESTIN HOTELS & RESORTS

Many of these luxury hotels offer senior rates but each has its own policy, so always ask about the possibilities when you make reservations. And if you are a member of United Silver Wings Plus, you will get your room at 50 percent off the published rate.

For information: Call 800-228-3000.

WINGATE INNS

A hotel chain with midscale prices for rooms with high-tech amenities, Wingate Inns gives a 15 percent discount off published room rates to members of a large number of senior organizations, including AARP, Catholic Golden Age, Retired Officers Association, and NARCUP, and anybody else who is over 60.

For information: Call 800-228-1000.

GOOD DEALS IN RESTAURANTS

Many restaurants offer special deals to people in their prime, but in most cases you'll have to seek them out yourself by reading the menu, asking at the restaurant, or watching the ads in the local newspapers. At some big chains, such as the International House of Pancakes, Kentucky Fried Chicken, Applebee's, and Wendy's, there's a recommended corporate policy of senior discounts or special senior menus that may or may not be followed at its franchised restaurants.

Sometimes a senior discount is available any time you decide to dine, but sometimes it's good only during certain hours, usually as "early bird" specials before 5 or 6 P.M. The eligible age varies from 55 to 65, and occasionally a restaurant requires that you sign up for its free senior club that issues you a membership card.

In addition, a few hotel chains will give you a break on your meal checks when you eat in their restaurants. For example:

At participating **Hilton Hotels** restaurants in the U.S. and Canada, you're entitled to a 20 percent discount on dinners for two, hotel guests or not, if one of you is a member of Hilton's Senior HHonors travel club.

Holiday Inn restaurants give a discount of 10 percent off your check when you dine there whether or not you are a guest at the inn if you belong to the Holiday Inn Alumni, a travel club for over-50s. On your birthday, your dinner will be free when another meal is purchased.

The restaurants in the participating **Marriott Hotels and Resorts** will take 20 percent off your bill for a party of up to eight people if you belong to AARP or CARP, whether or not you are guests of the hotel.

If you join the September Days Club, you'll get room discounts at **Days Inns** worldwide and also a minimum of 10 percent off meals at participating locations.

Doubletree Hotels and **Doubletree Guest Suites** take 10 percent off the bill for food and nonalcoholic beverages in participating restaurants for members of AARP who are guests at the hotel.

At most **Omni Hotels** you'll get 15 percent taken off the check for food and nonalcoholic beverages in the hotel restaurants by flashing your AARP card. The discount is yours at any hour if you are staying at the hotel, before 7 P.M. for dinner if you are not.

If you are a member of AARP or United Silver Wings Plus, you'll get a reduction of 15 percent on your food and beverage bills for yourself and your party when you eat at participating **Radisson Hotels Worldwide** restaurants, whether or not you are hotel guests.

Some of the restaurants at **Red Lion Inns** and **Thunderbird Motor Inns** will reduce your bill by 10 percent on food chosen from the regular menu, except on holidays, if you belong to AARP, CARP, or Mature Outlook. Be ready to produce your membership card.

WYNDHAM HOTELS & RESORTS

Different at each of the Wyndham Hotels & Resorts and Wyndham Gardens Hotels, the discounts offered to mature travelers amount to 20 to 50 percent off the regular room rates. This includes the Caribbean resort hotels as well as the other 60-or-so Wyndhams in the U.S. and Canada. To get the discount, ask for it when you make your reservations, mentioning that you belong to AARP or CARP or are over the age of 62.

For information: Call 800-WYNDHAM (800-996-3426).

11

Alternative Lodgings for Thrifty Wanderers

f you're willing to be innovative, imaginative, and occasionally fairly spartan, you can travel for a song or thereabouts. Here are some novel lodgings that can save you money and, at the same time, supply you with adventures worth talking about for years. They are not all designed specifically for people over 50, but each reports that a good portion of its clientele consists of free spirits of a certain age who are looking to beat the high cost of travel, meet people from other places, and have a real good time.

For more ways to cut travel costs and get smart in the bargain, check out the residential/educational programs in Chapter 16.

AFFORDABLE TRAVEL CLUB

Join this bed-and-breakfast club for mature travelers and you'll pay a pittance for accommodations, meet interesting people, and see new places. You may join as a host member, putting up other travelers in your spare bedroom a couple of times a year and providing breakfast and a little of your time to acquaint your guests with your area. Visitors pay $15 for a single or $20 for a double per night for their stay. In return, you get to stay in other people's homes for the same token fee when you travel. Or you may prefer to be a nonhost member, using the guest privileges only and paying $25 for a single or $30 for a double per night.

There are currently about 800 members in 45 states and 21 countries offering accommodations ranging from simple bedrooms to suites and condos. The annual host membership fee per household is $50, while a nonhost membership costs $90 a year. It entitles you to a quarterly newsletter and a directory that lists and describes the host homes. The club also sponsors a group tour once a year.

If you have a pet, you may want to take advantage of the club's new pet-sitting service—members move into your house and care for your pets while you're on vacation, meanwhile enjoying a visit to your neighborhood in exchange.

For information: Affordable Travel Club, 6556 Snug Harbor Ln., Gig Harbor, WA 98335; 206-858-2172.

COOPER COMMUNITIES

This group of six retirement villages located in Arkansas, Tennessee, South Carolina, and Missouri tempts potential residents to visit its planned communities by offering them inexpensive "Let's Get Acquainted" vacation packages. If you want to sample one of the villages, you may stay for one or more days for nothing or very little if you agree to take a sales tour around the property. For example, you may stay at one village for two nights and attend two shows for $29. Other properties charge from $18 for two nights to $50 per night. And one community offers complimentary lodging for up to three nights.

At most of the communities, the amenities include golf courses, tennis courts, hiking trails, boating, and recreation centers, all of which guests are invited to sample.

For information: Cooper Communities, 800-228-7328.

DEL WEBB'S SUN CITIES

Seven Sun Cities operated by the Del Webb Corporation offer Vacation Getaway programs designed as sample stays, just in case you're thinking of moving to one of these active adult communities. For remarkably little, you'll have your own villa for three, four, or seven nights starting any day of the week and enjoy all the facilities: tennis, golf, swimming, and socializing with residents and staff. Depending on the season and the location, the rates range from about $150 for three nights in the low season to about $575 for seven nights in the high season.

The only requirements are that one partner in a visiting couple is at least 55 years old and no one in your party is under 19. You also agree to accompany a salesperson on your own private tour of the property and listen to a sales presentation.

The communities currently offering Vacation Getaways include Sun City Grand in Phoenix, Sun City MacDonald Ranch and Sun City Summerlin in Las Vegas, Sun City Palm Desert in Palm Springs, Sun City Roseville in Sacramento, Sun City Hilton Head, and Sun City Georgetown in Austin, Texas.

For information: Del Webb Corporation, call 800-528-2604.

EVERGREEN BED & BREAKFAST CLUB

This is a bed & breakfast club for singles or couples over 50 who accommodate one another in their own homes. Members receive an annual directory that lists pertinent information about each host—occupation, interests, household pets, laundry privileges, and so on, plus nearby special attractions. Arrangements are made directly with the hosts. Whether or not a home is elegant or simple, the cost is only a modest gratuity payable to the host. Members may choose not to entertain guests, but many do. Those who do serve as hosts themselves pay $10 per day single, $15 per day double, to stay at the homes of other members. Those who prefer not to be hosts pay a little more per day, $18 for one or $24 for two.

The club has operated continuously since 1982 and now has more than 2,000 members, with 900 host locations in the United States and Canada. Annual club dues are $40 single and $50 double.

For information: Evergreen Club, PO Box 1430, Falls Church, VA 22041; 800-EVERGREEN (800-383-7473).

NEW PALTZ SUMMER LIVING

Think about spending a couple of the hottest months in the mountains, about 75 miles north of New York City. Every summer, while the usual student occupants are on vacation, 140 furnished garden apartments are reserved for seniors in the village of New Paltz, near Mohonk Mountain and home of a branch of the State University of New York. The rents at this writing for the entire summer (from early June until late August) range from $1,325 to $3,600, depending on the size of the apartment. Living right in town next to the campus, you may audit college courses free and attend lectures and cultural events. There is a heated pool and a tennis court in the complex, as well as a clubhouse. Buses travel to New York every Wednesday for those who want to go to the theater, and there are frequent day trips to places of interest.

For information: New Paltz Summer Living, 19 E. Colonial Dr., New Paltz, NY 12561; 800-431-4143 or 914-255-7205.

RETREAT CENTER GUEST HOUSES

If you are seeking a refuge from the pressures of daily life and time for quiet reflection, a stay at a retreat center may be your answer. Retreat centers are church-affiliated compounds where guests of any religious preference (or none at all) and of any age may find lodging and three meals for $35 to $45 a day. *U.S. and Worldwide Guide to Retreat Center Guest Houses* describes more than 850 such centers in the U.S., Canada, Europe, New Zealand, and Australia.

For information: CTS Publications, PO Box 8355, Newport Beach, CA 92660; 714-720-3729.

ROYAL COURT APARTMENTS

As an alternative to hotels, one-, two-, and three-bedroom apartments are available all year at the Royal Court in central London, one block from Hyde Park, giving you plenty of space and a home at the end of a busy day. You'll get a discount of 10 percent if you are over 50 and mention this book when you make your reservations.

For information: Royal Court Apartments, British Network Ltd., 594 Valley Rd., Upper Montclair, NJ 07043; 800-274-8583 or 201-744-5215.

SENIORS ABROAD

Seniors Abroad arranges for American seniors to spend three weeks in Japan, Australia, or New Zealand, staying with families there and learning about their lives and cultures. If you go, you'll stay for a week in each of three homes in different parts of the country you've chosen. You may also host visitors from foreign countries in your own home. All hospitality is voluntary on the part of the hosts and without cost to the guests, except for travel, tours, and hotel stays.

For information: Seniors Abroad, 12533 Pacato Circle North, San Diego, CA 92128; 619-485-1696.

SERVAS

Servas is an international cooperative system of hosts and travelers established to help promote world peace, goodwill, and understanding among peoples. A nonprofit, non-governmental, interracial, and interfaith organization open to all ages, it provides approved travelers with lists of hosts (and their special interests) all over the world, including the United States. To participate, you make your own arrangements to visit hosts, usually for two days at a time, in their homes. No money changes hands. The hospitable people who offer to share their space with you are eager to learn about you and your culture. You may do the same for other travelers in return, if you wish.

Travelers must pay a membership fee of $55 per year and are asked for two letters of reference and an interview. Hosts are interviewed and asked for a voluntary donation of $25 or more per year.

For information: Send a #10 self-addressed, stamped envelope to US Servas, 11 John St., Room 407, New York, NY 10038; 212-267-0252.

SUN CITY CENTER

Between Tampa and Sarasota, Florida, Sun City Center wants you to discover what a large, self-contained retirement town is all about and offers an inexpensive vacation package so you can sample the life there. You may stay for a few days or more. At this writing, a stay of four days/three nights with daily continental breakfast, tennis, swimming, and club facilities costs $89 per couple from April 15 through January 15 and $169 from January 16 through April 14. A round of golf costs extra, but this is the home of the Ben Sutton School of Golf and offers 126 holes. The only hitch: you must take a tour of the town accompanied by a salesperson.

For information: Sun City Center, PO Box 5698, Sun City Center, FL 33571-5698; 800-237-8200.

12

Perks in Parks and Other Good News

Here and there throughout the United States and Canada, enterprising officials in states, provinces, and cities have thought up some enticing ideas designed to capture the imagination of the mature population. Often they are expressing their appreciation of our many contributions to society and simply want to do something nice for us. And sometimes they are trying to lure a few of our vacation dollars to their vicinity, having discovered that we're always out for a good time and know a good deal when we see one.

But, first, keep in mind:

■ Before you set forth to visit a new area, it's a good idea to write ahead for free maps, calendars of events, booklets describing sites and scenes of interest, accommodation guides, and perhaps even a list of special discounts

159

or other good things that are available to you as a person in your prime.

■ Many states offer passes to their state parks and recreation facilities free or at reduced prices to people who are old enough to have learned how to treat those areas respectfully.

■ After the section on national parks, state park passes and other notable events are described for each state on the following pages. There may be other good deals that have escaped our attention, but those in this chapter are probably the cream of the crop.

ESCAPEES CLUB

Escapees is a club dedicated to providing a support network for RVers, full-time or part-time, most of whom are on the far side of 50. It publishes a bimonthly magazine filled with useful information for travelers who carry their homes with them, organizes rallies in the U.S., Canada, and Mexico, and hosts five-day seminars on RV living. Other benefits include discounted co-op RV parks and campgrounds, emergency road service, and mail/message services. After a $10 fee to join, the annual membership fee is $50 a year.

The club has recently established its own CARE Center (Continuing Assistance for Retired Escapees), a separate RV campground where retired members can live independently in their own RVs while receiving medical and living assistance, housekeeping, and transportation services as needed.

For information: Escapees Inc., 100 Rainbow Drive, Livingston, TX 77351; 888-757-2582 or 409-327-8873.

NATIONAL PARKS
GOLDEN AGE PASSPORT

Available for $10 to anyone over 62, this lifetime pass admits you free of charge to all of the federal government's parks, forests, refuges, monuments, and recreation areas that charge entrance fees. Anybody who accompanies you in the same noncommercial vehicle also gets in free. If you turn up at the gate in a commercial vehicle such as a van or bus, the passport admits you and your spouse, your children, and even your parents, so remember to take them along.

You will also get a 50 percent discount on federal use fees charged for facilities and services such as camping, boat launching, parking, or cave tours.

The passport is not available by mail. You must pick one up in person at any National Park System area where entrance fees are charged or at any offices of the National Park Service, the U.S. Forest Service, the Fish and Wildlife Service, or the Bureau of Land Management. You must have proof of age. A driver's license will do just fine.

(The free Golden Access Passport provides the same benefits for the disabled of any age. The Golden Eagle Passport, for those under 62, costs $25 per year.)

For information: National Park Service, PO Box 37127, Washington, DC 20013.

CANADIAN NATIONAL PARKS

The national parks and national historic sites throughout Canada charge modest entry fees for adults and take 25 percent off those for seniors. The same is generally true for provincial parks.

OFFERINGS FROM THE STATES

Virtually every state has a special senior rate for hunting and fishing licenses for people over a certain age (usually 65). Some states require no license at all for seniors, while others give you a reduced fee (usually half). Most require that you are a resident of the state to get these privileges. Most states also offer state park discounts to seniors, usually only residents, reducing or eliminating entrance fees and marking down camping rates. To check out the regulations in your state or a state you are visiting, call the state or local parks department or the state tourism office.

For a free listing of all the state tourism offices and their toll-free numbers, send a self-addressed, stamped envelope to Discover America, Travel Industry Association of America, 1100 New York Ave. NW, Ste. 450, Washington, DC 20005-3934.

CALIFORNIA

Campers 62 or over get $2 taken off admissions and overnight camping fees in state parks. Just show your ID at the gate.

For information: Call 800-444-7275 for campsite reservations.

If you are going to visit Newport Beach, ask for this city's free Visitor Information Pack, making sure to request the Senior Traveler Specials. This gives you a list of discounts and packages at hotels, early-bird dinner specials at restaurants, and free or discounted admission to museums, cruises, and other attractions.

For information: Newport Beach Conference and Visitors Bureau, 3300 W. Coast Hwy, Newport Beach, CA 92663; 800-94-COAST or 714-722-1611.

Is Long Beach your destination? Ask for the *Senior Saver Getaway Guide,* which lists the senior discounts at some of this city's hotels and attractions.

For information: Long Beach Area Convention and Visitors Bureau, 1 World Trade Center, Long Beach, CA 90831; 800-452-7829.

Carmel on the Monterey Peninsula also has some literature for you. It offers *Carmel's Escape for Seniors,* a free brochure describing a few discounts for people over the age of 55 at galleries, theaters, restaurants, shops, and accommodations. The catch: the discounts are not valid on Fridays or Saturdays or any time during July or August.

For information: Carmel Business Assn., PO Box 4444, Carmel, CA 93921; 800-550-4333 or 408-624-2522.

COLORADO

The Aspen Leaf Pass entitles Colorado residents 62 and over to free entrance to state parks any day and camping on weekdays. The pass costs $10 per year.

For information: Colorado Division of State Parks, 1313 Sherman St., Room 618, Denver CO 80203; 303-866-3437.

CONNECTICUT

Residents of Connecticut who are over 65 get a free lifetime Charter Oak Pass that gets them into state parks and forests plus Gillette Castle, Dinosaur Park, and Quinebaug

Valley Hatchery for free. In fact, their whole carload may enter the parks without charge. To get your pass, write to the address below and send along a copy of your current Connecticut driver's license.

For information: Charter Oak Pass, State Parks Division, DEP, 79 Elm St., Hartford, CT 06106-5127; 203-566-2304.

INDIANA

The Golden Hoosier Passport admits Indiana residents over the age of 60 and fellow passengers in a private vehicle to all state parks and natural resources without charge. An application for the Passport, which costs $5 a year, is available at all state parks or from the Indiana State Parks Department.

For information: Indiana State Parks Dept., 402 W. Washington St., Room W298, Indianapolis, IN 46204; 317-232-4124.

MAINE

Pick up your free Senior Citizen Pass and you will pay no day-use fees at Maine state parks and historic sites. The pass is available at any state park or by writing to the Bureau of Parks and Recreation and including a copy of a document that proves your age.

For information: Maine Bureau of Parks and Recreation, State House Station 22, Augusta, ME; 207-287-3821.

MICHIGAN

You can get some good deals in Michigan if you are a resident who's reached the age of 65. These include a motor-vehicle permit that gets you into all state parks for $5 a year, a fishing license with an annual fee of $1 a year, and a hunting license that costs $4 a year.

For information: Call the Department of Natural Resources at 517-373-9900.

MISSOURI

Missouri residents over the age of 60 are entitled to a free Silver Citizen Discount Card that gives them discounts at restaurants, stores, services, pharmacies, and other businesses throughout the state.

For information: Missouri Dept. of Social Services, PO Box 1337, Jefferson City, MO 65102-1337; 800-235-5503.

MONTANA

You need pay only half the usual camping fee in Montana's state parks if you are over the age of 62.

For information: Montana Fish, Wildlife, and Parks Dept., 1420 E. 6th Ave., Helena, MT 59620; 406-444-4041.

NEW HAMPSHIRE

Seniors Week at Mt. Washington Valley, in the White Mountains of New Hampshire, takes place every September just after Labor Day. Here, in the villages of Eaton, Conway, Pinkham Notch, North Conway, Bartlett, Glen, Madison, and Jackson, in this spectacularly beautiful high country, everyone over the age of 55 is entitled to discounted lodging prices (10 to 30 percent off), restaurant specials, retail discounts, and an array of events and activities.

For information: Mt. Washington Valley Visitors Bureau,

PO Box 2300, North Conway, NH 03860; 800-367-3364 or 603-356-3171.

NEVADA

In Carson City, you will strike silver without doing any digging—if you are over 50 and join the free Seniors Strike Silver Club. You'll get a list of varying discounts at hotels, motels, restaurants, museums, and shops here and in Virginia City plus a membership card to present as identification to participating merchants.

For information: Carson City Convention & Visitors Bureau, 1900 S. Carson St., Carson City, NV 89701; 800-NEVADA-1.

NEW MEXICO

For a list of senior discounts for attractions, stores, hotels, restaurants, and transportation in Albuquerque, call the toll-free number below.

For information: Albuquerque Convention & Visitors Bureau; 800-284-2282.

NEW YORK

Simply by presenting your current valid New York driver's license or a New York nondriver's identification card, you will be entitled to all of the privileges of the Golden Park Program for residents over the age of 62. The program offers, any weekday except holidays, free vehicle access to state parks and arboretums, free entrance to state historic sites, and reduced fees for state-operated swimming, golf, tennis, and boat rentals. Just show your driver's license or

ID card to the guard at each facility as you enter.
For information: State Parks, Albany, NY 12238; 518-474-0456.

OHIO

Residents of Ohio who are 60 or over may apply for a free Golden Buckeye Card, which entitles them to discounts, typically about 10 percent, on goods and services at thousands of participating businesses throughout the state. Applications are available at local sign-up sites.

For information and the sign-up site nearest your home: Golden Buckeye Unit, Ohio Dept. of Aging, 50 W. Broad St., 8th floor, Columbus, OH 43215-5929; 800-422-1976 or 614-466-3681.

PENNSYLVANIA

Send for a free brochure called *Mature Travelers Philadelphia Discounts* for a list of discounts available all year in this historic city. It lists dozens of Philadelphia sites and attractions, restaurants, hotels, tours, museums, theaters, and cultural events that offer special discounts for visitors over 50.

More good news for seniors in Philadelphia, whether visitors or residents, is the free transportation offered by SEPTA, the regional railway, bus, trolley, and subway system. If you are over 65 and have a Medicare, Railroad Retirement Annuity, or Senior Citizen Transit Identification card, you may ride free weekdays from 9 A.M. to 3:30 P.M., 6:30 P.M. to 6 A.M., and all day weekends and holidays. On the regional rail lines, you ride free or at reduced rates on all off-peak trains if you have the proper ID card.

For information: Philadelphia Visitors Center, 16th Street and JFK Blvd., Philadelphia, PA 19102; 800-537-7676. For information about SEPTA, call 215-580-7800.

The Pennsylvania Dutch country, which has become a favorite American tourist area, will send you a 36-page map and visitor's guide plus a free list of places—restaurants, hotels, motels, attractions—that offer discounts to seniors.

For information: Pennsylvania Dutch Convention and Visitors Bureau, 501 Greenfield Rd., Lancaster, PA 17601; 800-PA-DUTCH (800-723-8824).

SOUTH CAROLINA

The Golden Age Card is an identification pass for senior residents of South Carolina. It allows any resident over 65 free use of many facilities in state parks plus half off on camping fees.

For information: South Carolina Department of Parks, Recreation, and Tourism, 1205 Pendleton St., Columbia, SC 29201; 803-734-0166.

TENNESSEE

Travelers over the age of 62, residents of the state or not, are given 25 percent off the regular fees for camping in Tennessee's state parks and 10 percent off the room rates at the Resort Park Inns.

For information: Tennessee Tourist Development, PO Box 23170, Nashville, TN 37202; 615-741-2159.

GOOD SAM CLUB

The **Good Sam Club** is an international organization of RVers, mentioned here because the vast majority of people in rolling homes is over 50. This club can be handy and reassuring when you're cruising the country. Among its benefits are 10 percent discounts on nightly fees at over 1,700 RV parks and campgrounds, plus more discounts on propane, parts, and accessories at hundreds of RV service centers. In addition, the club offers a lost-key service, lost-pet service, trip routing, mail-forwarding, telephone-message service, insurance, a magazine, and campground directories. Very important, for an additional fee it provides emergency road service that includes towing for any vehicle, no matter the size. Also there are Good Sam rallies and travel tours all over the world, many of them "caraventures."

And not least, about 2,300 local chapters in the U.S. and Canada hold gatherings, meetings, and campouts. Membership per family is $25 for one year, $44 for two years.

For information: The Good Sam Club, 2575 Vista del Mar Dr., Ventura, CA 93001; 800-234-3450.

UTAH

The Silver Card issued by Park City, an old mining town known for its great ski mountains, is a free summer program of discounts that gives you 10 percent or more off on merchandise, tickets, and meals. Pick up your card at a participating hotel or the Park City Visitors Bureau. Plan to attend a Summer Senior Orientation and the annual Senior Picnic in the Park.

For information: Park City Convention and Visitors Bureau, 1910 Prospector Ave., Park City, UT 84060; 800-453-1360 or 801-649-6100.

VERMONT
Vermont's residents over 60 may purchase a Green Mountain Passport for $2 from their own town clerk. It is good for a lifetime and entitles them to free day-use admission at any Vermont State Park and its programs. Other benefits include discounts on concerts, restaurant meals, prescriptions, and more.

For information: Vermont Dept. of Aging, 103 S. Main St., Waterbury, VT 05676; 802-241-2400.

VIRGINIA
In this state that abounds with historical sites, you'll find senior discounts almost everywhere you go. You'll get them, for example, at Colonial Williamsburg, Busch Gardens, Berkeley Plantation, Mount Vernon, Woodlawn Plantation, Gunston Hall Plantation, the Edgar Allan Poe Museum in Richmond, and the Virginia Air and Space Center.

For information: Virginia Division of Tourism, 1021 E. Cary St., Richmond, VA 23219; 800-786-4484.

WASHINGTON, D.C.
The Golden Washingtonian Club is a discount program in the nation's capital for people over 60. With proof of age, both residents and visitors may get discounts from about 1,700 merchants listed in the *Gold Mine Directory*, free at many hotels or at the Washington Visitor Information Center. More than 30 hotels offer 10 to 40 percent off regular

rates, many restaurants take a percentage off meals, and many retail stores do the same for purchases.

For information: Family and Child Services of Washington, D.C., 929 L St. NW, Washington, DC 20001; 202-289-1510, ext. 120. To receive a copy by mail, send $2 handling fee.

WEST VIRGINIA

Everybody who turns 60 in West Virginia gets a Golden Mountaineer Discount Card, which entitles the bearer to discounts from more than 3,500 participating merchants and professionals in the state and a few outside of it. If you don't receive a card automatically, you may apply for one. Flash it wherever you go and save a few dollars.

For information: West Virginia Commission on Aging, 1900 Kanawha Blvd. East, Charleston, WV 25305; 304-558-3317.

13

Good Deals for Good Sports

Real sports never give up their sneakers. If you've been a physically active person all your life, you're certainly not going to become a couch potato now—especially since you've probably got more time, energy, and maybe funds, than you ever had before to enjoy athletic activities. Besides, you can now take advantage of some enticing special privileges and adventures offered exclusively to people over 49.

The choices outlined here are not for those whose interest in sports is limited to reclining in comfortable armchairs in front of television sets and watching football games, or settling down on hard benches in stadiums with cans of beer. They are for peppy people who do the running themselves.

Don't forget to check out the courses and trips included among Elderhostel's hundreds of low-cost residential academic programs. Here you will find many outdoor activities, such as golf, canoeing, hiking, skiing, biking, rafting, yoga, dance, tennis, spelunking, aerobics, and fly-fishing. Interhostel, too, schedules walking tours.

ELDERCAMP AT CANYON RANCH

ElderCamp is a seven-day health and fitness program for over-60s, offered twice a year at Canyon Ranch, an upscale fitness resort in Tucson. The purpose is to show you how to make positive changes in your lifestyle. A combination of education and exercise, the program includes daily aerobics and stretching; morning walks; sports; sessions with physicians, nutritionists, and therapists; relaxation instruction; group sessions on relevant issues; medical evaluations; and three healthy meals a day. Financial assistance is available for a limited number of participants for any life-enhancement wellness weeks, this one included.

For information: Canyon Ranch, 8600 E. Rockcliff Rd., Tucson, AZ 85750; 800-726-9900.

AMERICAN WILDERNESS EXPERIENCE

Action vacations are the specialty of AWE (see Chapter 3), an agency that offers trips from a great many tour operators (some mentioned separately in this book). You will get a choice of adventures ranging from horseback trips to sailing, canoeing, kayaking, hiking, trekking, dog sledding, scuba diving, biking, cross-country skiing, and other vigorous options, some of them specifically for people over 50.

For information: American Wilderness Experience, Inc., PO Box 1486, Boulder, CO 80306; 800-444-0099 or 303-444-2622.

OUTDOOR VACATIONS FOR WOMEN OVER 40

Any reader of this book is certainly over 40 and therefore qualifies, if female, for the trips organized by this adventure company for women who like to hike, bike, camp, ski, raft, and canoe with contemporaries. Trips are from only a couple of days to two weeks or even 17 days. Some are planned as multigenerational trips for mothers, daughters, grandmothers, granddaughters, aunts, and nieces; one participant must be over 40 and the other over 21. Accommodations vary from charming country inns, rustic lodges, and chateaus to windjammer bunks or sleeping bags under the stars.

Current adventures include a windjammer cruise in the British Virgin Islands; hiking and barging in Holland; hiking and rafting in Oregon; walking in England; hiking in Spain and Australia; kayaking, sailing, and camping in Baja; boating in Turkey; and cross-country skiing in Colorado.
For information: Outdoor Vacations for Women Over 40, PO Box 200, Groton, MA 01450; 508-448-3331.

THE OVER THE HILL GANG

This is a club that welcomes fun-loving, adventurous, peppy people over 50 (and younger spouses) who are looking for action and contemporaries to pursue it with. No naps, no rockers, no sitting by the pool sipping planter's punch. The Over the Hill Gang started as a ski club many years ago but its members can now be found participating in all kinds of activities. Recent trips have included skiing at Keystone, Taos, Steamboat, Vail, Big Sky, and other ski areas in the West, Val d'Isere in France, Valle Nevado in

Chile, and New Zealand. Plus whitewater rafting in Idaho, biking on Cape Cod and in Hawaii, rafting in the Grand Canyon, golfing in the Canadian Rockies.

The club currently has about 4,000 members in 50 states and 14 countries and 11 regional Gangs (chapters). Each local Gang decides on its own activities. If there's no chapter in your vicinity, you may become a member-at-large and participate in any of the activities.

The annual membership fee ($40 single, $66 for a couple) brings you a quarterly magazine, discounts, information about national and chapter events, and a chance to join the fun. The local Gangs charge small additional yearly dues.

For information: Over the Hill Gang International, 3310 Cedar Heights Dr., Colorado Springs, CO 80904; 719-685-4656.

BONUSES FOR BIKERS

Biking is becoming one of America's most popular sports, and people who never dreamed they could go much farther than around the block are now pedaling up to 50 miles in a day. That includes over-the-hill bikers as well as youngsters of 16, 39, or 49. In fact, some tours and clubs in the U.S. and Canada are designed especially for over-50s.

COUNTRYROADS BIKE TOURS

Biking in the Canadian province of Ontario is the specialty of this company whose escorted cycle holidays along quiet country roads in scenic areas include two-day midweek trips for bikers over 50. You'll lodge overnight in a country inn or B&B with a private bathroom. Among the senior bike trips are an exploration of Quinte's Isle in Prince Edward County, a ride in the Thousand Islands, and a spin through the farmlands and markets of Mennonite country. The tours are all-inclusive, bicycles and all.

Countryroads also hosts six-day Elderhostel bike tours of the same areas. For these, contact Elderhostel Canada. *For information:* Countryroads Bike Tours, PO Box 70657, 2938 Dundas St. West, Toronto, ON M6P 4E7; 416-536-1341.

THE CROSS CANADA CYCLE TOUR SOCIETY

This is a bicycling club for retired people who love to jump on their bikes and take off across the countryside. Most of the club's members are over 60, with many in their 70s and 80s and no one under 50. Says the society, "Our aim is to stay alive as long as possible." Now there's a worthwhile goal.

Based in Vancouver, B.C., with members—both men and women, skilled and novice—mostly in B.C., Ontario, and Alberta, it organizes many trips a year, all led by volunteer tour guides. Membership costs $25 single or $35 per couple and includes a bimonthly newsletter to keep you up to date on happenings. Several times a week, local members gather for day rides, and several times a year there are longer club trips to such far-ranging locations as the San Juan Islands, Waterton Park in Canada, and Glacier National Park in the U.S., Australia, Hawaii's Big Island, Arizona, New Zealand, and Denmark. Once a year a group of intrepid bikers pedals clear across Canada, an adventure that takes a few weeks to accomplish, with some members dropping in and out along the way. Many of the longer trips are tenting or camping tours, while others put you up in hostels, motels, or hotels.

For information: Cross Canada Cycle Tour Society, 6943 Antrim Ave., Burnaby, BC U5J 4M5; 604-433-7710.

ELDERHOSTEL'S INTERNATIONAL BICYCLE TOURS

Elderhostel, famous for its educational travel programs on the campuses of colleges and universities, also offers international bicycle tours that combine biking 25 to 35 miles a day with lectures by guides who accompany each trip and guest lecturers from local institutions. You bike as a group but at your own pace, with regular stops for tours, talks, site visits, snacking, and relaxing. Three-speed bikes are provided, as are breakfast and dinner. Accommodations are in clean, simple, double hotel rooms, most with private baths. A van travels with you to carry the luggage and bike equipment. It will also give you a ride if you decide you can't possibly make it up one more hill.

There are weekly departures hosted by IBT (see below) from April through September to England's East Anglia, Denmark, Austria, the chateaux country of France, and the tulip country in the Netherlands. The moderate cost covers airfare and just about everything else except lunches.

Elderhostel Canada's bike tours are hosted by Countryroads Bike Tours (check them out earlier in this chapter). At this writing, they include six-day itineraries both spring and fall: touring from Kingston to Ottawa; rambling through Prince Edward County, and pedaling through Mennonite country.

For information: Elderhostel, 75 Federal St., Boston, MA 02110; 617-426-7788. In Canada: Elderhostel Canada, 308 Wellington St., Kingston, ON K7K 7A7; 613-530-2222.

INTERNATIONAL BICYCLE TOURS

The Fifty Plus Tour run by IBT is planned for people over 50 who are not into pedaling up mountains but love to cycle. The trip goes to Holland in May and takes you on a leisurely trip along bicycle paths and quiet country roads on flat terrain through farmland and quaint villages. You'll cover only about 30 miles a day, so there is plenty of time for sightseeing, snacking, shopping, and relaxing. Although this is the only tour strictly limited to over-50s, many older bikers are found on IBT's other bike tours to Holland, Denmark, England, Ireland, Italy, France, Bermuda, Austria, Cape Cod, Charleston, the Chesapeake and Ohio Canal, and Florida. And, of course, many more sign on for Elderhostel's bike tours (in England, France, the Netherlands, Austria, and Denmark), all hosted by IBT.

For information: International Bicycle Tours, PO Box 754, Essex, CT 06426; 860-767-7005.

SENIOR WORLD TOURS

Pedaling at a leisurely pace through some of the country's most beautiful areas, you have time to savor the scenery and historic sights. This agency's tours, which are specifically for mature bikers, currently include a trip on rolling rural roads in the San Juan Islands in the Puget Sound, an exploration of the bluegrass country of Kentucky, and a walking/rafting/biking tour of Yellowstone and Grand Teton National Parks.

For information: Senior World Tours, 2205 N. River Rd., Freemont, OH 43420; 888-355-1686.

WANDERING WHEELS

A program with a Christian perspective and "a strong biblical orientation," Wandering Wheels operates long-distance bike tours for all ages in this country and abroad, including a 40-day, 2,600-mile Breakaway Coast-to-Coast every spring that's geared specifically for people who are "middle age or older." And there is a week's trip every September in a different locale.

For information: Wandering Wheels, PO Box 207, Upland, IN 46989; 317-998-7490.

TENNIS, ANYONE?

An estimated four million of the nation's tennis players are over 50, with the number increasing every year as more of us decide to forego rocking chairs for a few fast sets on the courts. You need only a court, a racquet, a can of balls, and an opponent to play tennis, but, if you'd like to be competitive or sociable, you may want to get into some senior tournaments.

UNITED STATES TENNIS ASSOCIATION

The USTA offers a wide variety of tournaments for players over the advanced age of 35, at both local and national levels. To participate, you must be a member ($25 per year). When you join, you will become a member of a regional section, receive periodic schedules of USTA-sponsored tournaments and events in your area for which you can sign up, get a discount on tennis books and publications, and receive a monthly magazine and a free subscription to *Tennis* magazine.

In the schedule of tournaments, you'll find competitions listed for specific five-year age groups: for men from 35 to 85-plus and for women from 35 to 80-plus. There are also self-rated tournaments that match you up with people of all ages who play at your level. If you feel you're good enough to compete, send for an application and sign up. There is usually a modest fee.

For information: USTA, 70 W. Red Oak Lane, White Plains, NY 10604-3602; 914-696-7000.

USTA LEAGUE TENNIS, SENIOR DIVISION

If you want to compete with other 50-plus tennis players in local, area, and sectional competitions on four different surfaces culminating in a national championship, join the Senior Division of the USTA League Tennis program. Your level of play will be rated in a specific skill category ranging from beginner to advanced, and you'll compete only with people on your own ability level. Sign up in your community or write to the USTA for details.

For information: USTA, 70 W. Red Oak Lane, White Plains, NY 10604-3602; 914-696-7000.

USTA PLAY TENNIS AMERICA

The USTA Play Tennis America program is designed to encourage adult beginners, especially those over 50, to learn how to play the game. Available in many communities all over the country in public parks and tennis clubs, this is a three-stage instructional program, with each stage lasting three weeks (three hours a week). Stage 1 teaches basic tennis skills; Stage 2 provides ongoing review and drills; Stage 3 introduces low-key competition in preparation for possible participation in USTA Senior Leagues. The cost is inexpensive and loaner racquets are available.

For information: USTA, 70 W. Red Oak Lane, White Plains, NY 10604-3602; 914-696-7000.

VAN DER MEER TENNIS UNIVERSITY

Van der Meer Tennis University offers inexpensive five-day Seniors Clinics regularly from August to May every year, most at its center on Hilton Head Island but a few in Lakeland, Florida. Specifically for 50-plus players, beginning or experienced, the clinics provide more than 16 hours of instruction, including video analysis, tactics and strategies for singles and doubles, match play drills, plus round robins, social activities, and free court time. The goal is to improve your strokes and game strategy and show you how to get more enjoyment out of your game. Discounted accommodations are available for participants. If you attend a clinic on a nonsenior week or weekend, you will get a 10 percent discount by showing your AARP card.

For information: Van der Meer Tennis University, PO Box 5902, Hilton Head Island, SC 29938-5902; 800-845-6138 or 803-785-8388. In Lakeland: 800-270-1999.

WALKING TOURS

There are so many organizations offering walking/hiking trips designed for or eminently suited to mature travelers that we can't list them all here. The following, however, specialize in travel on foot. Other walking trips are mentioned throughout the book. Get yourself in shape for the hikes by walking 10 miles or more every week for at least a month.

APPALACHIAN MOUNTAIN CLUB

Every year this famous hiking club schedules a few treks, of two or more days, for people over 50 who hike in these lush mountains and valleys by day and sleep in rustic mountain huts by night. The hikers have time to savor the scenery and the glorious views, and get a glimpse of the area's wildlife. The hikes vary from year to year and sometimes include trips for 50-plus women only and a Silver Sneakers Weekend in New Hampshire during fall foliage season.

For information: Appalachian Mountain Club, 20 Joy St., Boston, MA 02108; 617-523-0636.

ELDERTREKS

On these trekking trips in exotic lands, most of them in the Far East, you will hike overland on foot and, in many cases, sleep on an air mattress in a tribal village house or a tent. The trips are rated for difficulty so you may choose one that matches your abilities. For more, see Chapter 5.

For information: ElderTreks, 597 Markham St., Toronto, ON M6G 2L7; 800-741-7956 or 416-588-5000.

INTERHOSTEL

Interhostel's collection of educational trips for people over 50 now includes a couple of walking programs, one in Bordeaux and the Dordogne Valley of France, the other in the Tuscany region of Italy. Moving from place to place by van or bus, you'll set forth on foot to explore, taking leisurely walking tours wherever you go. You'll cover perhaps three to five miles a day, sometimes on unpaved, uneven rocky terrain with stairs and moderate hills, so be sure you are an enthusiastic walker. See Chapter 16 for more about Interhostel programs.

For information: Interhostel, University of New Hampshire, 6 Garrison Ave., Durham, NH 03824; 800-733-9753 or 603-862-1147.

SENIOR WORLD TOURS

If you are an energetic person in your prime, consider the walking tours this agency plans specifically for you. One trip takes you to the Inside Passage of Alaska, where you'll explore by foot and ferry. Others ramble through Utah's Bryce Canyon and Zion National Parks, Washington's Olympic Peninsula, France's Dordogne River Valley, England's Cotswolds, and California's wine country. The tours are six or seven days, allowing for leisurely walks on gentle or moderate terrain so that you'll have an opportunity to savor the scenic countryside. Lodging is in small inns or guesthouses.

For information: Senior World Tours, 2205 N. River Rd., Fremont, OH 43420; 888-355-1686.

SHOTT'S WALKS IN THE WEST

On these guided walking trips exclusively for people over the age of 50, you'll explore places you'd never see from a car or a bus, have close encounters with the wilderness, and get your exercise. But you won't be spending the nights in a sleeping bag under the stars—you'll sleep in a comfortable bed in a lodge or a motel, complete with bathroom. Recent walks have taken place in Arches and Canyonlands National Parks, Olympic National Park, the San Diego coastal area, the Colorado Rockies, and Death Valley. One trip a year, usually in Alaska, is designated for you and your grandchildren over the age of 18.

Trips are limited to six guests per guide and you carry only your own day pack. Can you keep up? If you can walk comfortably for about 10 miles a week, you're in shape for these hikes.

For information: Shott's Walks in the West, PO Box 51106, Colorado Springs, CO 80949; 719-531-9577.

SIERRA CLUB

Don't sign up for the club's backpacking trip in the Carson-Iceberg Wilderness in California if you have lived the life of a couch potato, advises the Sierra Club. That's because even though it is for grandparents and their grandchildren, it is definitely strenuous. If you still want to know about it, you'll find more information in Chapter 3.

WALK YOUR WAY

The walking tours led by Rosemary Davenport in her native England always include a few trips a year designated for seniors. These are 12-day tours of quaint and picturesque places on the Isle of Wight, the Devon coast, the Dales of Yorkshire, and the Cotswolds. These are circular walks covering only a few miles a day, staying in one location and visiting a different village every day, with frequent stops to take in the sights and scenery.

Although some of the tours for all ages are fairly strenuous, many of them are also eminently suitable for mature walkers who are in good enough shape to cope with more miles and a few ascents. On these, you'll walk a total of 50 miles or more (seven or eight miles a day), lodge in bed & breakfasts or small inns along the way, and eat hearty pub food.

For information: Walk Your Way, PO Box 231, Red Feather Lakes, CO 80545; 970-881-2709.

WALKING THE WORLD

Anyone who loves adventure, is at least 50 years old, and is in good physical shape is invited to participate in Walking the World's explorations. These are 7- to 17-day backcountry treks, covering 6 to 10 miles a day, that focus on natural and cultural history. On some trips, you'll camp out and, carrying only a day pack, hike to each new destination. On others, you will lodge in cabins, small country inns, or B&Bs, setting forth on daily walks into the countryside. Groups are small, from 12 to 18 participants plus two local guides, and there's no upper age limit. No previous hiking experience is necessary, but obviously you need to be in good physical shape.

Destinations include Arches and Canyonlands National Parks in Utah; Banff and Jasper National Parks in the Canadian Rockies; plus trips in Scotland, England, Wales, Switzerland, Ireland, New Zealand, Maine, Hawaii, Costa Rica, and Italy.

For information: Walking the World, PO Box 1186, Fort Collins, CO 80522; 800-340-9255 or 970-225-0500.

MOTORCYCLE HEAVEN
BEACH'S MOTORCYCLE ADVENTURES

If motorcycling is your passion and adventure is in your blood, look into motorcycle tours offered by the Beaches, a family that's been conducting cycling tours since 1972. All ages, including yours, may choose among several itineraries including the Alpine Adventure through the mountains of Germany, Austria, Italy, Switzerland, and France, and the Maori Meander in the backcountry of New Zealand. Other trips are planned for Norway and South Africa. Motorcycles, all BMWs, are provided in your choice of available models and there is no mileage charge. Your luggage is carried by a van. By the way, both bikes and automobiles are welcome on these tours, so if friends or family want to join you they may go along in a car.

You're on your own during the day, following a tour book that gives daily itineraries, road maps, distances, estimated en route times, business hours, sight-seeing ideas, good (and bad) roads, suggestions for activities, driving tips, and directions to the hotel of the night. The daily routing, pace, and stops are up to you. There are several riding options for each day, so you may decide to cruise along or ride long and hard. Every evening, however, you'll meet the group and your guide at a comfortable hotel or family farm where you'll eat dinner that night and have breakfast the next morning.

For information: Beach's Motorcycle Adventures, 2763 W. River Parkway, Grand Island, NY 14072; 716-773-4960.

RETREADS MOTORCYCLE CLUB

Retreads, motorcycle enthusiasts who have reached the ripe old age of at least 40, get together for state, regional, and international rallies to talk cycling and ride together. Their theme song? "On the Road Again." Each state association also schedules weekly or monthly gatherings. Started as a correspondence club in 1969, it has grown to over 25,000 members—men and women—in the U.S., Canada, and several other countries including Japan, England, and Australia. Annual contribution is $10 a year per person or $15 per couple. A club newsletter keeps members informed of the activities.

For information: Retreads Motorcycle Club International, 528 North Main St., Albany, IN 47320; 317-789-4070.

CANOE VACATIONS

GUNFLINT NORTHLAND OUTFITTERS

These outfitters, with paddling adventures on the remote lakes of the Boundary Waters Wilderness Area between Minnesota and Ontario, the largest waterways wilderness in the world, schedule several one-week trips every summer expressly for seniors. With a guide, you paddle and portage your canoe deep into heavily forested areas, home to moose, beaver, mink, loons, and other creatures of the wild. One option is a seven-night package limited to eight guests that includes two nights at Gunflint Lodge and five nights camping with complete outfitting. Camp is set up for you, and your meals—perhaps including the fish you've caught—are cooked over the campfire by your guide. The second choice is a lodge-to-lodge trip that combines three nights at the Lodge, one night at a rustic inn on an island across the border in Canada, and the others exploring and camping in the wilderness. Yet another option is gathering a few friends and setting up your own special trip.

For information: Gunflint Northwoods Outfitters, 750 Gunflint Trail, Grand Marais, MN 55604; 800-362-5251.

ELDERHOSTEL

Some of the programs offered by Elderhostel include canoeing in their course offerings. Recently, for example, canoeing has been one of the curriculum choices for wilderness trips in Maine and Colorado.

For information: Elderhostel, 75 Federal St., Boston, MA 02110; 617-426-7788.

BARGE TRIPS

LANAKAI CHARTER CRUISES

A 15 percent discount is yours if you travel the canals of France aboard a 94-foot barge that accommodates your own party of six passengers in three cabins, each with private bath, and a crew of three. That is, it's yours if one of your group is over 50. Depending on the week you choose, you may float through the Ardennes or Champagne regions, Burgundy, the Loire Valley, or perhaps the Seine and Yonne Rivers. You travel at a nice slow pace, covering 50 to 100 kilometers a day, with time to explore on foot, mountain bike, or, escorted by crew members, in a van.

Breakfast and lunch are served on board, dinner ashore. *For information:* Lanakai Charter Cruises, 98-985 Kaonohi St., Aiea, Hawaii 96701; 800-487-6630 or 808-487-6630.

KAYAKING TOURS
NEW ZEALAND ADVENTURES

Here's your chance to take a five-day sea kayak tour among the six main islands in the Bay of Islands in New Zealand. This is a relaxed tour specifically for you and your peers over 50, and the only criteria for participation is that you are in good health and love an active vacation. You'll stay in a cabin in Otehei Bay on Urupukapuka Island, eat home-cooked meals, and travel with a knowledgeable local kayak guide who is your age. You'll spend your days exploring the volcanic rock formations and sea caves by kayak (paddling perhaps three to five miles a day), taking day hikes on island trails, swimming, snorkeling, sailing, and becoming acquainted with the Maori culture. Trips are scheduled in our winter, New Zealand's summer.

For information: New Zealand Adventures, HCR 56 Box 575, John Day, OR 97845; 541-932-4925.

GOLFING VACATIONS
GREENS FEES

Most municipal and many private golf courses offer senior golfers (usually those over 65) a discount off the regular greens fees. Take your identification with you and always make inquiries before you play.

BERMUDA SENIOR GOLF CLASSIC

Open to men and women 50 and over, the Senior Golf Classic is a week of tournament golf and parties. It includes five nights at a choice of three resort hotels, three rounds of golf on three different golf courses, one practice round, cocktail parties, a banquet with prizes, and time off to explore the island.

For information: Senior Classic Tournament, PO Box GE 304 St. George's GE BX, Bermuda; 441-297-8148.

GOLF ACADEMY OF HILTON HEAD ISLAND

If you have an American Express Senior Member Card (see Chapter 10), you may sign up for the Golf Academy's three- or four-day golf schools at Sea Pines Plantation in Hilton Head and get a 15 percent discount on the cost. You'll get instruction on everything from full swings and chipping to flop shots, and play 18 holes at the Harbour Town Golf Links.

For information: Golf Academy of Hilton Head Island, PO Box 5580, Hilton Head Island, SC 29938; 800-925-0467.

THE GOLF CARD

This card, designed especially for senior golfers with lots of time to play on every possible golf course, costs $95 the first year for a single membership or $145 for two and thereafter $85 for a single and $135 for a double per year. It entitles you to two complimentary 18-hole rounds or up to 50 percent off players' fees at each of nearly 3,000 member golf courses throughout the world.

Membership benefits include a Quest International card

that gives you up to 50 percent discounts on hotels and motels, the *Golf Traveler* magazine, which contains a directory and guide to the participating courses and resorts, and discounts at many resorts when you book golf travel packages.

The average member of this group is 61 years old and has played golf for 24 years, plays 81 rounds a year, travels 11 weeks a year, travels with a spouse, and plans golf as an important part of his or her leisure travel.

For information: The Golf Card, PO Box 7020, Englewood, CO 80155; 800-321-8269 or 303-790-2267.

NATIONAL SENIOR SPORTS ASSOCIATION (NSSA)

More than 3,000 golfers over 50—average age 63—belong to the NSSA which sponsors recreational and competitive four-day midweek golf holidays once a month at highly rated courses all over the country. The holidays include accommodations, golf (including a 54-hole medal tournament), breakfasts, at least two dinners, and activities for nonplaying companions. Recent locations have included Pebble Beach in California, Kings Mill Resort in Williamsburg, the Homestead at Hot Springs, Barton Creek in Austin, TX, and the Sagamore in Bolton Landing, NY. Longer golf holidays are scheduled once a year to more far-flung locations such as Ireland and England, Portugal, Mexico, Canada, and Hawaii.

Membership in NSSA costs $25 a year, includes your spouse, entitles you to participate in the trips, and gets you a voluminous monthly newsletter. It also includes a $100 certificate to use toward your first trip of the year and a Golf Passport for free rounds on courses around the country.

For information: NSSA, 301 N. Harrison St., Princeton NJ 08540; 800-282-6772.

JOHN JACOBS GOLF SCHOOLS

Golfers over the age of 62 get a discount of 10 percent on the cost of golf vacations offered July through December at any John Jacobs Golf School. You'll learn how to improve your game while you play at some of the finest courses in the country. Most packages include lodging, breakfast and dinner, instruction, course time, greens fees, and cart.
For information: John Jacobs Golf Schools, 800-472-5007.

LEARNING ADVENTURES GOLF CLINIC

If you want to improve your game, sign up for the golf clinic tailored specifically for players in their prime offered by Learning Adventures. This 10-day educational travel program is sponsored by the College of the Tehachapis in California and combines daily practice at several courses near Bakersfield with professional instruction on all aspects of the game from tee to cup. An inexpensive holiday, it includes accommodations and all meals.
For information: COTT, PO Box 1911-61, Tehachapi, CA 93581; 805-823-8115.

TOUR NEW ZEALAND

Twelve-day golf tours in New Zealand for travelers over the age of 60 and their younger spouses are offered every winter (summer in that part of the world). Tour New Zealand package trips include airfare, accommodations with breakfast, sight-seeing tours, and eight days of golf. You'll play on several different courses on the two major islands.

For information: Tour New Zealand, 150 Powell St., San Francisco, CA 94102; 800-822-5494 or 415-421-3171.

EVENTS FOR RAPID RUNNERS
FIFTY-PLUS FITNESS ASSOCIATION

This is not a club, although it occasionally sponsors athletic events for its over-50 members. It is an organization formed by eminent exercise researchers at Stanford University for the exchange of information about physical exercise and its benefits (and hazards) among the older population. Its members, from almost every state and several foreign countries, also serve as volunteers for ongoing studies of such activities as running, swimming, biking, and racewalking. Each is asked to contribute $25 a year, tax-deductible, to defray costs. The association sponsors many events in the California Bay area. These include walks, runs, swims, bike rides, seminars and conferences on aging.

For information: Fifty-Plus Fitness Association, PO Box D, Stanford, CA 94309; 415-323-6160.

OVER-50 SOFTBALL
NATIONAL ASSOCIATION OF SENIOR CITIZEN SOFTBALL

The NASCS is an association of several thousand softball players and hundreds of teams in the U.S. and Canada, with a goal of promoting a worldwide interest in senior softball. To play ball on one of its teams, you must be at least 50 years old. There's no upper age limit, and both men and women are welcomed. NASCS is the organizer of the annual Senior Softball World Series, a tournament for players who must first qualify in local competitions. Every year more than 100 teams from the U.S. and Canada compete in a major ballpark. A quarterly magazine keeps members up to date on happenings here and abroad.

For information: NASCS, PO Box 1085, Mt. Clemens, MI 48046; 810-792-2110.

SENIOR SOFTBALL USA

This organization conducts softball tournaments all over the country and organizes international tournaments as well, including the Senior Softball World Championship Games held in September. Anyone over 50, man or woman, in the U.S. and Canada may join and many thousands have. Members get assistance finding teams in their areas and may subscribe to the *Senior Softball USA News*, which keeps them up to date on tournaments and other news. They are eligible to take part in an annual international tour that takes teams to play ball in foreign lands.

For information: Senior Softball USA, 9 Fleet Ct., Sacramento, CA 95831; 916-393-8566.

NATIONAL SENIOR GAMES

U.S. NATIONAL SENIOR SPORTS ORGANIZATION

The USNSO, sponsored by major corporations, promotes health and fitness for seniors through competitive multisport events held across the country, including the National Senior Sports Classic–Senior Olympics, a national competition that occurs every two years. In May 1997, it's at the University of Arizona in Tucson. In 1999, it will be at Walt Disney World in Orlando.

To qualify for the more than 500 separate events—in track and field, swimming, cycling, golf, tennis, bowling, volleyball, horseshoes, archery, 5- and 10-kilometer runs, badminton, softball, racquetball, racewalking, 3-on-3 basketball, triathlon, shuffleboard, and table tennis—athletes must first qualify in authorized state competitions across the country. The events are organized for men and women in five-year age brackets from 50 to 100-plus.

If you want to be ready to go for the next senior games, get the ground rules from your local senior sports organization or the national headquarters.

For a free list of local and state games all over the country, contact USNSO at the address below. You'll find a representative sample of these games in the following pages. *For information:* USNSO, 1307 Washington Ave., St. Louis, MO 63103; 314-621-5545.

STATE AND LOCAL SENIOR GAMES

Most states hold their own senior games once or twice a year and send their best competitors to national events. If you don't find your state among those listed here, that doesn't mean there's no program in your area—many are sponsored by counties, cities, even local agencies and colleges. Check with your local city, county, or state recreation departments to see what's going on near you or contact the USNSO for a free list. You don't have to be a serious competitor to enter these games but merely ready to enjoy yourself. So what if you don't go home with a medal? At the very least, you'll meet other energetic people and have a lot of laughs.

ARIZONA

If you are over 50, male or female, you are eligible to participate in the Flagstaff Senior Olympics held over four days every year in September. You may compete in events that include bowling, cycling, golf, handball, racewalking, swimming, tennis, track and field, powerlifting, and more. Sign up for the festivities, which include an evening social and tickets to a Northern Arizona University football game. Medals are awarded for each event.

For information: Flagstaff Senior Olympics, PO Box 5063, Flagstaff, AZ 86011-5063; 520-523-3560.

CALIFORNIA

Hundreds of senior athletes from all over the United States and Canada compete every winter in the annual California Senior Olympics–Palm Springs. The sporting events range from track and field to golf and tennis, with medal winners going on to compete in the National Senior Olympics. If you are 50 or more, a resident or a visitor to the state, you are eligible to participate.

For information: California Senior Olympics–Palm Springs, Mizell Senior Center, 480 S. Sunrise Way, Palm Springs, CA 92262; 619-323-5689.

On the last weekend in February each year, the Running Springs Senior Winter Games are held at Running Springs, a resort at an elevation of 6,500 feet in the San Bernardino National Forest. Open to anyone over the age of 50, the competitions include skiing, ice skating, ice fishing, snowball throwing, snowshoe racing, and a few indoor games such as billiards, bridge, and table tennis. Social events are included. There is a modest registration fee plus a small additional fee for each event entered.

For information: Running Springs Senior Winter Games, PO Box 3333, Running Springs, CA 92382; 909-867-3176.

COLORADO

The Senior Winter Games at the Summit take place each year during three days in the second week of February in the quaint Victorian village of Breckenridge. Anyone from anywhere who's over 55 and wants to compete against peers is welcome. Events include cross-country skiing, downhill slalom, speed skating, snowshoe races, biathlon, figure skating, and more, plus social activities. Age categories for the competitions begin at 50 to 54 and increase in five-year increments to 90-plus. A registration fee that allows you to participate in as many events as you wish currently stands at $15.

The summertime Rocky Mountain Senior Games take place in Greeley, Colorado, every August and include many events ranging from running to swimming, dancing, and tennis.

For information: Senior Winter Games at the Summit, PO Box 442, Breckenridge, CO 80424; 970-453-2461. Or for the Rocky Mountain Senior Games: Rocky Mountain Senior Games, 1010 6th St., Greeley, CO 80631; 970-350-9433.

CONNECTICUT

The Connecticut Senior Olympics include not only competitive sport events but also a mini health fair and many physical fitness activities. Residents of Connecticut and neighboring states who are 55-plus converge on the University of Bridgeport on the first weekend in June for three days of events such as the 5,000-meter run, the 100-yard dash, the mile run, the long jump, diving, bocci, and tennis. These summer games require a small entrance fee.

The one-day Connecticut Senior Winter Olympics, usually held in March, are open to anyone from anywhere who's 55 and an amateur. The games feature downhill, giant slalom, cross-country, and snowshoe races, and take place at Ski Sundown.

For information: Connecticut Senior Olympics, 380 University Ave., Bridgeport, CT 06601; 203-576-4722. Or for the winter games: Connecticut Senior Winter Olympics, PO Box 208, New Hartford, CT 06057; 203-379-9851.

FLORIDA

The Golden Age Games in Sanford are the biggest and the oldest Senior Games in the country. Held annually in November, they go on for a week and include plenty of competitions, ceremonies, social events, and entertainments. If you are over 50, you are eligible to participate regardless of residency. In other words, you needn't be a Florida resident to compete for the gold, silver, and bronze medals in such sports as basketball, biking, bowling, canoeing, checkers, diving, dance, swimming, tennis, triathlon, track and field, canasta, and croquet. There is a small entry fee for each event.

For information: Golden Age Games, PO Box 1298, Sanford, FL 32772; 407-330-5699.

Palm Beach also has big games every year. Called the U.S. Senior Athletic Games, they are open to anyone 50 or older and feature competitions in everything from biking to bowling, racquetball, golf, swimming, tennis, running and walking races, track and field events, and a beauty contest. You will compete within your own five-year age range.

For information: U.S. Senior Athletic Games, 200 Castlewood Dr., North Palm Beach, FL 33408; 407-842-3030.

MICHIGAN

Michigan Senior Olympics, a four-day happening open to people 50 and older, are held every year on the campus of a state college. For small registration and event fees, you get a chance to compete for medals in athletic events from archery to volleyball. You may also take home ribbons for your baking skills, arts and crafts, and dancing. Spectators are welcomed too.

For information: Michigan Senior Olympics, 312 Woodward, Rochester, MI 48307; 810-608-0250.

MISSOURI

The St. Louis Senior Olympics have become an institution in Missouri by now. A four-day event that is open to anyone who lives anywhere and is 50 years old, it costs a nominal amount and is action-oriented. No knitting contests here—only energetic events such as bicycle races, 200-meter races, standing long jumps, golf, basketball, tennis singles and doubles, and swimming.

For information: Senior Olympics, JCCA, 2 Millstone Campus, St. Louis, MO 63146; 314-432-6780, Ext. 188.

MONTANA

Men and women over the age of 50, from Montana or other states, are invited to participate in the Montana Senior

Olympics. Held every year, this event moves to another city every third year. Events range from archery, badminton, and basketball to swimming, tennis, and volleyball.

For information: Montana Senior Olympics, 465 Freedom Ave., Billings, MN 59105; 406-252-2795.

NEW HAMPSHIRE

For three days in September, you can compete with your peers in the Granite State Senior Summer Games, which feature 15 sports events ranging from swimming to tennis, track and field, shuffleboard, and table tennis. In alternate years, these are qualifying games for the U.S. Senior Sports Classic. Sign up if you are at least 50 and in good operating condition. The cost is minimal. Regional games are also scheduled throughout the state during the summer.

The Granite State Senior Winter Games, held in Waterville Valley for three days in March, are open to men and women 50 and over who compete in groups of five-year increments. They get a chance to challenge their peers in dual slalom, giant slalom, and cross-country races. Other events include speed skating, snowball throw, hockey goal shoot, and snowshoe races. Everyone in the appropriate age range is welcome to enter the competitions and attend both an opening reception and an awards banquet. Costs for entry, lift tickets, fees, rentals, and social affairs are low. Inexpensive lodging is also available.

For information: Granite State Senior Winter Games, PO Box 1942, Rochester, NH 03866; 603-332-0055.

NEW YORK

The Empire State Senior Games, open to all New York residents who are 50 or over, are held in Syracuse over three days in June. Winners may qualify for the National Senior Olympics. For a small registration fee, amateur athletes may compete in many events that range from swimming to bridge, basketball, softball, croquet, track and field, tennis, race walking, cycling, and more. There are additional fees for golf and bowling. Participants are invited to social events each of the three nights.

For information: Empire State Senior Games, NYS Parks, 6105 E. Seneca Turnpike, Jamesville, NY 13078; 315-492-9654.

NORTH CAROLINA

After local games are held statewide, the winners travel to Raleigh for the North Carolina Senior Games State Finals and, perhaps, on to the national games. Most sports are on the agenda, plus an arts competition that celebrates artists in heritage, literary, performing, and visual arts. The state also sponsors the SilverStriders, a walking club for those 50 or better that gives its members log books for tracking progress, gifts and awards, and an annual report of their accomplishments.

For information: North Carolina Senior Games, PO Box 33590, Raleigh, NC 27636; 919-851-5456.

PENNSYLVANIA

The Keystone Senior Games "combine sports, recreation, and entertainment with fellowship." You can get some of each if you are a Pennsylvania resident who is 50 or older. The games are held over five days in July at a university campus where you can get lodging and three meals a day at low cost. If you prefer to stay in a motel, you'll get a senior discount.

For information: Keystone Senior Games, 31 S. Hancock St., Wilkes Barre, PA 18702; 717-823-3164.

VERMONT

If you are over 50 and an amateur in your sport, you are invited to participate in the Green Mountain Senior Games. At the summer games held in September at Green Mountain College in Poultney, the competitive events—organized in age groups from 50 to 100-plus—include everything from golf and tennis to swimming, darts, horseshoes, walking, running, table tennis, bowling, croquet, softball, and shuffleboard. And just for fun, there are scenic walks, socials, and free swims.

The Green Mountain Cross-Country Senior Games take place in February at Blueberry Lake, in Warren, VT. You may compete in Nordic skiing, snowball throwing, and snowshoe competitions.

For information: Green Mountain Senior Games, 131 Holden Hill Rd., Weston, VT 05161; 802-824-6521.

VIRGINIA

Virginia's Golden Olympics are an annual four-day event held each spring on a college campus, where older athletes compete to qualify for the U.S. National Senior Olympics— or just for the fun of it. It is a combination of social events and entertainment with sports competitions, open to Virginia residents over the age of 55. Spouses are invited to come along and enjoy the hospitality, which includes parties, dances, tours of local sites, and other festivities. The fees are low, lodging and meals are cheap, and the sporting events are many, ranging from rope jumping, miniature golf, and riflery to swimming, running, and tennis for age groups from 55 upwards.

For information: Golden Olympics, James City Parks and Recreation, 5249 Olde Towne Rd., Williamsburg, VA 23188; 804-565-6920.

14

Adventures on Skis

▣VER THE TOP ON TWO NARROW BOARDS

Downhill skiing is one sport you'd think would appeal only to less mature, less wise, less breakable people. On the contrary, there is an astounding number of ardent over-50 skiers who would much rather glide down mountains than sit around waiting for springtime. In fact, many of us ski more than ever now that we're older because we can go midweek when the crowds are thinner and we get impressive discounts on lift tickets. And a lot of us are taking up the sport for the first time. Ski schools all over the United States and Canada are reporting an increase of older students in beginner classes.

The truth is, you're never too old to learn how to ski or to improve your technique. Once you get the hang of it, you can ski at your own speed, choosing the terrain, the difficulty level, and the challenge. You can swoop down cliffs through narrow icy passes or wend your way down gentle slopes in a more leisurely fashion, aided by the new improved skis and boots, clearly marked and carefully groomed trails, and sophisticated lifts that take all the work out of getting up the mountain.

Besides, ski resorts are falling all over themselves catering to older skiers, offering discounts, cheap season passes, and other engaging incentives. In fact, it is a rare ski area that does not give a break to skiers over a certain age.

CLUBS FOR MATURE SKIERS
THE OVER THE HILL GANG

OTHG began as a ski club (three former Colorado ski instructors were looking for company on the slopes), and skiing is still its major activity. If you are 50, you are eligible to join (your spouse may be younger) and enjoy the club's ski adventures on this continent and abroad. You pay special group rates and sometimes receive free guides and special lift-line privileges. In addition, at many ski areas, even when you ski on your own you will get "senior" discounts like those offered skiers over 65 on lift tickets, rentals, lessons, and packages. People who have never put on a pair of skis or haven't tried them in years can take advantage of Learn to Ski programs, refresher clinics, or group lessons.

Every year OTHG schedules at least 20 escorted Senior Ski Week packages in the U.S. West, Europe, Canada, New Zealand, and South America. And when the ski season ends, you may join the Gang for a bike trip, a party, whitewater rafting, hiking, or golfing. This club, with an average age of 64, is definitely out for a good time.

Local OTHG chapters also run their own ski trips and all members everywhere are invited to go along. At some ski areas, local and visiting members meet once a week to ski together. At Breckenridge in Colorado, for example, they gather on Tuesdays to ski all day with their own guides and get together for lunch. At Keystone, it's every Thursday morning, and at Vail, Monday is the day for camaraderie.

National membership requires an annual fee of $40 ($66 per couple) plus chapter dues if you join a local Gang. *For information:* Over the Hill Gang International, 3310 Cedar Heights Dr., Colorado Springs, CO 80904; 719-685-4656.

SENIOR SKIER NETWORK

A group of 50 resorts throughout the East has joined together to offer midweek senior skier programs modeled after the Senior Skier Development Program at Ski Windham in New York. Each host mountain welcomes everybody over 50 to its full-day program, which includes clinics and ski instruction with four hours of on-snow lessons and other activities that vary from mountain to mountain. Cost is more than a lift ticket but less than a lift/lesson combination. Many of these areas also offer a Senior Program Package for the season. Each area's program feeds into the winter state games in Vermont, Connecticut, Massachusetts, and New York.

The same organization, PSIA-E/EF, that created the Senior Skier Network also presents the one-day Senior Winter Games held at Ski Windham in February. They are open to anyone who is over 50 and skis, no matter how well. The games include a NASTAR slalom, obstacle, team relay, and other snow activities.

In addition, there's a race-training clinic for senior skiers of all skiing levels. The clinic features instruction and presentations from top people in racing and recreational skiing.

For information: Professional Ski Instructors of America, Eastern Education Foundation, 1-A Lincoln Ave., Albany, NY 12205-4900; 518-452-1166.

70+ SKI CLUB

You must prove you are 70 before you can join this club that now has almost 12,500 members, all of them in their 70s, 80s, and 90s. The club meets at ski areas for races, companionship, and partying and also organizes big trips in the U.S. and other parts of the world.

Lloyd T. Lambert, a former ski columnist who was born in 1901, founded the 70+ Ski Club in 1977 with 34 members. Its primary purpose was to make skiing less expensive for older people on limited incomes, and the campaign worked. Today most ski areas give over-70s free or half-price lift tickets. Says Lambert, "We provide inspiration to the 50-year-olds who think they're too old to ski."

Hunter Mountain, in New York's Catskills, hosts the club's annual meeting every year in early March. This is when the 70+ Ski Races are held, an event so popular that the contestants are divided into three age groups: men 70 to 80, women 70 to 80, and everyone over 80. There are serious slalom races with awards presented at a gala party at the lodge.

Most gatherings take place in New York state and New England, but there are always at least a couple of adventures in the Alps, the Rockies, or even Australia, New Zealand, and Argentina. The club has members in all parts of the United States and Canada as well as Europe.

Lifetime membership costs $5 ($15 if you live outside of the U.S. or Canada). Proof of your date of birth is required with your application, and you may not apply more than two weeks before your 70th birthday. You will receive a 70+ Ski Club patch, a newsletter that tells you about upcoming events, and a list of ski areas where you can ski free or at substantial discounts.

For information: Lloyd T. Lambert, 70+ Ski Club, 104 Eastside Dr., Ballston Lake, NY 12019; 518-399-5458.

THE WILD OLD BUNCH

This merry band of senior skiers who navigate the steep slopes of Alta in Utah is an informal group of men and women from Utah and many other states who ski together for fun, welcoming anybody who wants to join them. There are no rules, no designated leaders, no lessons, no regular meetings, and no age restrictions, though most members are well past 50, retired business or professional people. Somewhere between 50 and 100 avid skiers now wear the Wild Old Bunch patch.

The group grows haphazardly as members pick up stray mature skiers they find on the slopes, showing them their mountain and passing along their enthusiasm for the steeper trails and the off-trail skiing in Alta's famous powder. Says a spokesperson, "If you visit Alta and would like to join in some of the old-fashioned camaraderie of skiing, just look for any of us on the slopes or on the deck of the mid-mountain Alpenglow Inn, where we gather for lunch and tales. Either ski with us or grab a seat for some lively conversation."

Although the bunch isn't sexist, some of the wives prefer to stay on less difficult slopes or to travel the cross-country trails, so they wear "Wild Wives" patches.

For information: Look for the Wild Old Bunch on the slopes.

MORE GOOD DEALS FOR DOWNHILL SKIERS

The older you are, the less it costs to ski. There's hardly a ski area in North America today that doesn't give mature skiers a good deal. Many cut the price of lift tickets in half at age 60, others do it at 65, and most stop charging altogether at 70. A few areas charge anybody over the age of 65 only $5 a day to ski, and most make offers on season passes that are hard to refuse. Others plan special senior programs specifically for mature skiers.

To give you an idea of what's out there, here is a sampling of the special senior programs, workshops, and clubs in the states where skiing is big business. This list does not include all areas, of course, so be sure to check out others in locations that interest you. Remember to carry proof of age with you at all times. The ski areas change their programs every year or so, too; so, using the following information as a guide, you must do some of your own research.

CALIFORNIA

Ski in California and you'll get good deals on lift tickets and season passes almost everywhere. Plus, there are some special programs designed especially for mature skiers, such as the following.

Tahoe Donner Downhill Ski Area schedules ski clinics for skiers over the age of 50 every Tuesday morning. The inexpensive package for beginners and experienced skiers includes a lift ticket, continental breakfast, three hours of ski lessons and a videotape review of your skiing technique.

At Northstar-at-Tahoe, the three-day Golden Stars Clinic has been tailored for skiers over 60 of intermediate or better ability who want to improve their skills on the slopes. Offered several times a winter, the clinic provides three-hour morning lessons, all-day lift tickets, and video analysis.

A special program for intermediate and advanced skiers over 40 who need to learn better technique and style is offered for only $12 on weekends and holidays at Kirkwood Ski Resort.

And at Squaw Valley, anybody over 60 may ski all day for only $5.

The senior program at Bear Valley, in the Sierra Nevada Mountains between Lake Tahoe and Yosemite, is even better. At 65, you may ski free any day, any time. If you prefer a season pass, you can get one for just $10.

COLORADO

Every ski area in Colorado offers discounted lift tickets to seniors, some starting at 60, others at 65. Most charge nothing at all to ski after 70. And there are many special programs, lessons, and clubs especially designed for mature skiers. For example:

At Breckenridge, two-day 50-Plus Seminars for seniors of all skiing abilities, taught by seniors, include a full-day lesson each day, video analysis, and a group dinner. Breckenridge is the place where members of the local Over The Hill Gang, plus any other visitors 50 and over, get together on Tuesdays for a day on the slopes with their own guide. Breckenridge also hosts the Senior Winter Games at the Summit for three days in February.

It's Thursday mornings at Keystone for Gang members and visitors to ski with volunteer guides. Members of AARP and OTHG also get a 30 percent discount on lodging at Keystone with a 60-day advance reservation.

At Vail, any skier over 50 is welcome to meet on Mondays and ski with OTHG members. At Steamboat, together with volunteer guides, they gang up on the slopes every day from Sunday through Thursday. At all of the mountains, all 50-plus skiers, members or not, are invited along.

Silver Creek Resort offers Never-Ever 50+, a learn-to-ski program exclusively for mature people who have never been on skis before. Scheduled on Wednesday and Saturday mornings, it includes lesson, equipment, and lift ticket.

Sunlight Mountain Resort in Glenwood Springs has its 100 Club, open to couples whose combined ages total 100 years or more, or singles who are 50 or older. Club members meet each Wednesday to ski in the morning and stay for lunch.

Crested Butte Mountain, too, has one-day senior workshops for beginners to advanced skiers, and a senior women's group called the Crested Butte Beauties welcomes visitors and locals. At Eldora, skiers and snowboarders 65 and older can participate in Senior Ski every Tuesday. Senior Days at Ski Cooper gives you a day lift ticket, free racing and an après-ski party. Telluride's Master Club race program for seniors meets on Saturdays for lessons on gate training, carving techniques, and speed.

The SnoMasters Classic at Purgatory, for skiers 55 and over, is a four-day event held twice every winter, providing discounted lessons by instructors of your own generation, breakfast each morning, and a party.

IDAHO

At the famous Sun Valley, two weeks in January are Prime Time Weeks when skiers over 60 get discounted lift tickets and accommodations, plus lots of special events including a big band dinner dance, an après-ski pub crawl, NASTAR races, and a mountain tour.

Schweitzer Mountain's Prime Timers Club for skiers 55 and over is an informal club whose members ski together almost every day and get together for social gatherings every Thursday afternoon. In addition, there's a bargain senior ski week in March, the Snowmaster's Classic, a week of workshops, clinics, social activities, and race training for older skiers who are seeking to improve their technical abilities.

MAINE

At Sunday River Ski Resort, those who purchase the Perfect Turn Gold Card or Platinum Card and are 50 or over are eligible for unlimited membership in the Prime Time Club. The club skis together with an instructor on Tuesday and Thursday mornings. The cards also entitle participants to other privileges as well.

At Sugarloaf/USA, a Perfect Turn Platinum Card is what you need to participate in the Prime Time Club for skiers over 50. At this ski area, the senior clinic meets for lessons on Tuesday and Thursday afternoons.

MICHIGAN

At Crystal Mountain Resort, every Tuesday is Silver Streak Day when skiers over the age of 55 are entitled to free group lessons. At Caberfae Peaks, Silver Streak Day is on Thursdays when you may ski all day for $12 if you are over 50. And, if you are over 55, check out Senior Week, held every January at Sugar Loaf Resort. You'll get half-price skiing, a good deal on accommodations, and free NASTAR.

NEVADA

At Mt. Rose, just outside of Reno, skiers over 50 are welcomed every Friday morning for coffee and a free two-hour mountain clinic with senior instructors.

NEW HAMPSHIRE

It's a rare ski area in this state that doesn't offer older skiers a good break on lift tickets at age 65 or so, and a free pass at 70. Many also have special programs targeting seniors. Here's a sampling:

Waterville Valley's Silver Streaks, a club for skiers who have passed their 55th birthdays (and spouses at any age), has several enticements. Mondays through Thursdays, you get reserved parking, coffee and pastries in the base lodge, and a guided warm-up run, reduced-price NASTAR on Wednesdays, and Silver Streak instructional clinics throughout the season. Cost is nominal.

At Attitash Bear Peak, TGIF (Thank Goodness I'm Fifty) meets Thursdays for a ski clinic that includes fitness workshops, coffee and doughnuts, discount lessons, special races, and an end-of-the-season party.

Every Friday morning for 10 weeks, the Heritage Ski Club meets at Mt. Cranmore for group lessons. You qualify if you are over 60.

Loon Mountain's Flying 50's Plus meets every Thursday and Friday mornings for two-hour lessons.

The Senior Cruisers, 50 plus, meet Monday mornings at Cannon Mountain and Wednesdays at Mt. Sunapee, for two hours with instructors.

The Mountain Meisters, again for skiers over 50, gathers on Thurdays at Gunstock for skills clinics and video analysis. Special events include a recreational race day, equipment demo day, first tracks, and a race.

And at Temple Mountain, the Morning Birds, a seven-week program for seniors, runs Monday through Friday with lessons on skis or snowboards.

NEW MEXICO

What senior skiers get almost everywhere in New Mexico are reduced fees for lift tickets at 62 or 65 and, in some areas, free skiing at 70. And at Taos Ski Valley, in the San-gre de Cristo Mountains, a program for skiers over 50 is offered four times per season. The package includes group lessons, lift tickets, video analysis, racing, and social events.

NEW YORK

Skiers over 50 are invited to join the Ski Windham Senior Skier Development Program for 6 or 10 consecutive Tuesdays, January through mid-February, all at moderate cost. You may attend the program by the day, if you prefer. What you get is morning coffee, presentations on ski-related subjects, daily lift tickets, four hours of on-snow instructions, and workshops.

UTAH

Virtually all of Utah's ski areas give senior skiers reduced rates on lift tickets at 60 or 65, with Sundance and Elk Meadows offering free rides to those over 65. Most others stop charging at 70—except Alta where you must wait until you are 80!

At Snowbird, the Silver Wings program offers full-day classes on negotiating the slopes to intermediate-and-above skiers 55 and up. And a four-day senior seminar is scheduled once every winter.

Alta's Alf Lingen Ski School gives special three-hour Silver Meisters lessons designed specifically for mature skiers who need to brush up their skills.

As for Brighton Ski Resort, there's the Seniors' Workshop for skiers over 50 on three consecutive Wednesdays that includes lessons, breakfast, and a social hour.

VERMONT

Vermont's ski areas were the first to cater to older skiers and it is highly unlikely that there are any resorts there that don't give seniors a decent break on lift tickets and season passes. Along with special rates, several areas offer special senior programs as well. Here's a sample.

At Jay Peak any skier over the age of 55 is invited to

join the Silver Peaks Club, a group that skis together every Tuesday. For a nominal daily fee, you are entitled to a day on the slopes, a guided tour, coffee and doughnuts, and après-ski activities. If you're past 65, you may ski here any time for $5 a day.

The It'SnoWonder is a club for skiers over 55 at Smuggler's Notch, offering its members skiing every Wednesday, plus coffee and doughnuts, savings on rental equipment and group ski lessons, 50 percent off day ticket rates, mountain tours, videotaped skiing, afternoon get-togethers with speakers, discussions, and a farewell barbecue. Membership fee is $10 for the season.

Cranmore Mountain's Heritage Program for senior skiers features three hours of instruction every Friday.

And here's the deal at Stowe: The 50+ Friday Ski Club meets every Friday in January and February for four hours of instruction and a hot chocolate break for $50 plus a lift ticket.

OTHER SKI ADVENTURES
SKI NEW ZEALAND

Four times a year, Ski New Zealand plans ski trips to this faraway country especially for over-50s (and younger companions). Scheduled in our summer months—New Zealand's winter—the 14-day packages take you to seven different resorts in New Zealand's Southern Alps. The packages include airfare from Los Angeles, accommodations, ground transportation, free stopovers, and sightseeing. Sign up early and you may stop over at no extra cost in Australia, Tahiti, Fiji, or Hawaii. Mention this book.

For information: Ski New Zealand, 150 Powell St., San Francisco, CA 94102; 800-822-5494 or 415-421-3171.

SKIING WITH ELDERHOSTEL

Many Elderhostel programs hosted by colleges and other institutions offer downhill ski instruction to beginners and intermediates over the age of 55 (and their younger companions). Just like other Elderhostel adventures, they are inexpensive and always combine the skiing with lectures and classes, lodging, and meals. All are listed in the voluminous catalogs sent out regularly by this organization. See Chapter 16.

For information: Elderhostel, 75 Federal St., Boston, MA 02110; 617-426-7788.

CROSS-COUNTRY SKIING

Many cross-country areas also give senior skiers a break. Always ask about discounts before paying admission, because you may save a few of your hard-earned dollars.

ELDERHOSTEL

Elderhostel, known for its low-cost learning vacations for people over 55 (and companions who may be younger) at educational institutions (see Chapter 16), has combined cross-country skiing and winter nature exploration since 1978. Since the programs change from year to year, you must check out the offerings in its catalogs.

For information: Elderhostel, 75 Federal St., Boston, MA 02110; 617-426-7788.

OUTDOOR VACATIONS FOR WOMEN

Hook into this agency (see Chapter 3) for cross-country ski adventures with instruction in such locations as Crested Butte, Colorado. For women who live near Boston, there are weekend trips to nearby ski resorts in Vermont.

For information: Outdoor Vacations for Women Over 40, PO Box 200, Groton, MA 01450; 508-448-3331.

FOR SNOWMOBILE ENTHUSIASTS

SENIOR WORLD TOURS

You must be at least 50 to ride snowmobiles into Yellowstone National Park and a sleigh through the National Elk Refuge on these six- to eight-day tours scheduled every winter by Senior World Tours. Limited to 30 people, the trips are based at Cowboy Village Resort at Togwotee, 50 miles out of Jackson Hole, Wyoming. Snowmobiles, snowmobile suits with boots and helmets, and most meals are included. No expertise is required, but don't even think of it unless you're in good physical condition.

For information: Senior World Tours, 2205 N. River Rd., Fremont, OH 43420; 888-355-1686.

15

Back to Summer Camp

aybe you thought camp was just for kids, but if you are a grown-up person who likes the outdoors, swimming, boating, birds, and arts and crafts and appreciates fields and forests and star-filled skies, you too can pack your bags and go off on a sleepaway. Throughout the country, many camps set aside weeks for adult sessions, while others offer adult programs all season long. More and more adults are getting hooked on summer camp, and many wouldn't miss a year.

ELDERHOSTEL
Many of Elderhostel's programs are a combination of camping and college. In this wildly successful low-cost educational program (see Chapter 16 for details), you can spend a week or two camping in remote scenic areas, enjoying all the activities from horseback riding to crafts, boating,

campfires, and sleeping in a cabin or under the stars. *For information:* Elderhostel, 75 Federal St., Boston, MA 02110; 617-426-7788. In Canada: Elderhostel Canada, 308 Wellington St., Kingston, ON K7K 7A7; 613-530-2222.

RV ELDERHOSTELS

Less expensive than regular Elderhostel programs because you take along your own housing, these programs come in two varieties. One is the usual Elderhostel educational vacation on a college campus, where you partake of the happenings, including courses, meals, and excursions, with the rest of the group but sleep in your own RV, trailer, or tent on the campus or at nearby campgrounds. The other is a mobile program or moving field trip—in Alaska, for example, Wyoming, the Yukon, or along the Oregon Trail—where you'll hear the lectures over your CB radio as you travel. Moving along like a wagon train, you travel in a group led by an experienced guide and make many stops for lectures and sightseeing as you go.

For information: Elderhostel, 75 Federal St., Boston, MA 02110; 617-426-7788. In Canada: Elderhostel Canada, 308 Wellington St., Kingston, ON K7K 7A7; 613-530-2222.

GRANDPARENTS/GRANDCHILDREN CAMP

See Chapter 3 for information about summer camps and other vacations designed to give grandparents and grandchildren some special time together.

THE SALVATION ARMY

The Salvation Army operates scores of rural camps across the country, most of which have year-round adult sessions.

The camps are run by regional divisional headquarters of the Army; thus each is different from the others. Open to anyone, they cost very little.

For information: Contact a local unit of the Salvation Army.

VOLUNTARY ASSOCIATION FOR SENIOR CITIZEN ACTIVITIES

VASCA is a nonprofit organization that will provide you with detailed information about camps in the New York area for people over the age of 55. The agency represents 11 vacation lodges scattered about New York, New Jersey, Connecticut, and Pennsylvania, all of them amazingly affordable. Some are small rustic country retreats, most are lakeside resorts, others are huge sprawling complexes with endless activities. Several are designed to accommodate the disabled and the blind as well as the very elderly. The camps are sponsored by various nonprofit organizations and foundations, some with religious affiliations but nonsectarian.

For information: VASCA, 281 Park Ave. South, New York, NY 10010; 212-645-6590.

YMCA/YWCA

The Y runs many camps, most of them for children, but some also offer inexpensive weeks for adults. For example, the YMCA of the Rockies operates a resort, Snow Mountain Ranch, with a special program in mid-August for active adults over the age of 50 at its Camp Chief Ouray in Granby, CO. Activities during the week's program include swimming, hiking, tennis, archery, biking, animal watches, dancing, and more. The High Point YMCA's Camp Cheerio in the Appalachian Mountains of North Carolina sets aside three weeks a year for campers over 50, who live in the same cabins and pursue the same activities as the kids do the rest of the summer.

For information: Call your local YMCA or YWCA for information about camps in your area.

CAMPS SPONSORED BY CHURCH GROUPS

There are many camps and summer workshops sponsored by religious organizations, too many and too diverse to list here. One source of information is Christian Camping International, which offers an inexpensive guide that lists 850 camps and conferences in the U.S.

For information: Christian Camping International/USA, PO Box 62189, Colorado Springs, CO 80962-2189; 719-260-9400.

AUDUBON ECOLOGY CAMPS

Not for over-50s alone, these are included here because mature nature lovers will enjoy these natural-history programs for adults run by the National Audubon Society. There are three Audubon Ecology Camps for grown-ups (in Wyoming, Maine, and Connecticut) where the outdoors is used as a classroom for six-day sessions during the summer months. Here you live on-site while you learn all about the surrounding environment, from marine and island ecology to mountain, meadow, woods, and water habitats.

For information: National Audubon Society, 613 Riversville Rd., Greenwich, CT 06831; 203-869-2017.

16

Going Back to School After 50

ave you always wanted to learn French, study African birds, examine Eskimo culture, delve into archaeology, international finance, horticulture, the language of whales, or great literature of the 19th century? Now is the time to do it. If you're a typical member of the over-50 generation, you're in good shape, healthy and alert, with the energy and the time to pursue new interests. So why not go back to school and learn all those things you've always wished you knew?

You are welcome as a regular student at just about any institution in the United States and Canada, especially in the continuing-education programs, but many colleges and universities have set up special programs designed to lure older people back to the classroom. Some offer good reductions in tuition (so good indeed that sometimes you may attend regular classes half price or even free) and give credits for life experience. Others have designed programs, and sometimes whole schools, specifically for mature scholars.

Going back to class is an excellent way to generate feelings of accomplishment and to exercise the mind—and one of the best ways to make new friends. It doesn't necessarily mean you'll have to turn in term papers or take excruciatingly difficult exams. Sign up for one class a week on flower arranging or Spanish conversation or a once-a-month lecture series on managing your money. Or register as a part-time or full-time student in a traditional university program. Or take a learning vacation on a college campus. Do it *your* way.

You don't even have to attend classes to learn on vacation. You can go on archaeological digs, count butterflies, help save turtles from extinction, brush up on your bassoon playing, listen to opera, search for Roman remains in Europe, study dancing or French cuisine, or go on safari in Africa.

EDUCATIONAL TRAVEL PROGRAMS

ELDERFOLK

Each of Elderfolk's two- to five-week courses in Nepal, India, Tibet, Bhutan, China, and Pakistan focuses on Himalayan culture, history, natural history, religion, and arts and crafts. Several provide close looks at the native cuisines, and many include trekking. Exclusively for adventurers over the age of 55, they are offered by the Folkways Institute, which also plans study courses for students and professors.

Some of the courses, combining education and exotic travel, are cultural treks on which you'll be put up at night in roomy tents or lodges. Others are residential or overland trips where you lodge in small hotels or guest houses. Check out the Overland Journeys for Elderfolks—for example, the Ancient Silk Road trip, tracing Marco Polo's route from Beijing to Rawalpindi.

No previous knowledge or training is required, but some stamina definitely is.

For information: Folkways Institute, 14600 SE Aldridge Rd., Portland, OR 97236-6518; 800-225-4666 or 503-658-6600.

A WEEK IN THE MOUNTAINS

Explore is a learning vacation in early fall for "active mature adults" over the age of 50. Set in Beaver Creek, in Vail Valley, Colorado, it offers symposia, hands-on workshops, and outdoor recreational clinics mixed with social activities and exercise. The sessions focus on a choice of topics from global political issues to art, history, geology, and astronomy. Workshops may include such subjects as wildlife photography, astronomy, and gourmet cooking, while the outdoor clinics range from fly fishing to golf dynamics.

For information: Explore, NorthStar Institute, 312 S. Franklin St., Denver, CO 80209; 800-298-4242 or 303-777-6873.

ELDERHOSTEL

Elderhostel, the educational travel program for mature people, offers some of the world's best bargains. Astonishingly inexpensive and infinitely varied, Elderhostel's short-term academic programs number in the thousands. They are hosted by over 2,000 educational and cultural institutions in every U.S. state and Canadian province as well as 70 foreign countries. The idea is to sign up for a program in a place you want to visit offering courses you want to take. The only requirement for participation is that you must be 55 or over. Your accompanying spouse may be any age, but another companion must be at least 50.

Started in the mid-70s when some colleges wanted to make use of their facilities, empty dorms, and teaching talent during summer vacations, Elderhostel programs are now offered all year. The organization acts as a clearinghouse for the host institutions, each of which designs its own programs that include three academic classes taught by the faculty and may use the Elderhostel name if they meet certain criteria.

On domestic Elderhostels, the programs usually start on a Sunday afternoon and last five or six nights. The typical cost is around $330, including accommodations, meals, five days of classes, and a variety of extracurricular activities. Foreign trips, more expensive, include airfare and are two to four weeks long. In most cases, you'll lodge on college or university campuses and enjoy the cultural and recreational resources that go with them. You'll take three courses taught by the faculty, but there are no exams, grades, or homework, nor do you get college credits for them. The accommodations are plain but comfortable, the food institutional but nourishing. There are usually two twin beds to a room, with a bathroom down the hall. And there is no maid service. On the other hand, the setting is often beautiful, the courses interesting, and the company remarkably varied.

The course offerings are myriad. Look through the voluminous catalogs published every season for state-by-state and country-by-country listings of host institutions and the classes they offer. Or view them on the Internet or at your public library.

Some of the domestic programs include sports and adventures, from canoeing to skiing, hiking, biking, and more. Overseas, there are walking trips in Switzerland and bike trips in Austria, Denmark, England, France, and the Netherlands. And a new Homestay program lets you live with a foreign family for one week out of a two-week trip.

If you'd like to contribute your time, energy, and expertise to a volunteer organization that provides significant services all over the world, look into the Elderhostel Service Program (see Chapter 18). Elderhostel has joined forces with many national nonprofit organizations to create service opportunities for people over 55.

If you want to take your adult children or grandchildren along, you'll find intergenerational programs as well (see Chapter 3).

There is sure to be a program somewhere in a place you've always wanted to visit, giving courses you've always wanted to take, at any time of the year. Ask to be placed on the mailing list for the seasonal catalogs.

For information: Elderhostel, 75 Federal St., Boston, MA 02110; 617-426-7788. In Canada: Elderhostel Canada, 308 Wellington St., Kingston, ON K7K 7A7; 613-530-2222.

ELDERTREKS

The exotic adventures planned by ElderTreks to places such as China and Tibet, Thailand, and Borneo qualify as travel/study trips because they immerse you in the cultures you visit. See Chapter 5 for more.

For information: ElderTreks, 597 Markham St., Toronto, ON M6G 2L7; 800-741-7956 or 416-588-5000.

INTERHOSTEL

An international study/travel program for energetic people over the age of 50 (a companion need be only 40), Interhostel is sponsored by the University of New Hampshire. It offers more than 75 one-week and two-week learning vacations each year around the world, from Africa to Finland, Australia, New Zealand, Asia, the French West Indies, and South America, about which its three free catalogs a year will keep you posted. The idea is to stay in one country long enough to become well acquainted with the place you are visiting. During your stay, you will be introduced to the history, culture, and people through lectures, field trips, sightseeing excursions, and social and cultural activities. Your group, from 25 to 40 participants, will be accompanied by a representative of the university. Trips are scheduled year-round and are cosponsored by educational institutions in the host countries.

Living quarters, clean and comfortable although not necessarily fancy, are in residence halls or modest hotels. Most meals are cafeteria-style and feature the local food of the region. The cost, moderate for what you get, includes full room and board, tuition, airfare, and ground transportation.

Because Interhostel's adventures impose a busy schedule of activities, you should be healthy and fit, full of vim and vigor, able to climb stairs, tote your own baggage, and walk comfortably at a moderate pace for more than a mile at a time. This is especially important if you join one of Interhostel's new walking programs (see Chapter 13).

For information: Interhostel, University of New Hampshire, 6 Garrison Ave., Durham, NH 03824; 800-733-9753 or 603-862-1147.

SAGA HOLIDAYS

Saga Holidays, marketing travel only for people over 50, offers travel/study programs as well as myriad escorted tours and cruises. One is its own series of Smithsonian Odyssey Tours and another is the Road Scholar program, with itineraries that feature educational themes. The programs include expert lecturers, selected literature, and predeparture educational materials. See Chapter 5 for more.

For information: Saga Holidays, 222 Berkeley St., Boston, MA 02116; 800-343-0273; Smithsonian Odyssey tours: 800-258-5885. Road Scholar Program: 800-621-2151.

HOSTELSHIPS

Elderhostel offers a limited number of full or partial scholarships, to be used only in the U.S., for people who find the tuition costs of the programs beyond their means. Funds to cover travel costs are not included and eligibility is determined upon completion of an application that includes a confidential questionnaire. Scholarship programs in Alaska and Hawaii are available only to residents of these states.

For information: Write to Elderhostel, 75 Federal St., Boston MA 02110. Attention: Hostelships.

SENIOR VENTURES

A network of colleges and universities in four western states—Oregon, Washington, Arizona, and Texas—offers people over 50 a chance to combine education with recreation and travel. College-level courses taught by faculty members offer everything from trout fishing to Shakespeare, interfaith studies, Southwestern archeology, computer skills, the Oregon Trail, river rafting, Southwestern ecology, and more. Most of the programs, which vary in length from one to four weeks, take place on college campuses and feature expeditions and field trips, but some take you on international adventures to such faraway places as Turkey, Scotland, and Alaska. Moderate fees cover virtually everything.

For information: Senior Ventures Network, Siskiyou Center, Southern Oregon State College, Ashland, OR 97520-5050; 800-257-0577.

TRAVELEARN

The upscale learning vacations by TraveLearn take small groups of adults all over the world, putting you up in first-class or deluxe accommodations and providing faculty escorts chosen from a nationwide network of more than 280 cooperating universities and colleges, as well as local lecturers, in each place you visit. You'll learn through on-site lectures, seminars, meals with local families, visits to homes and workplaces, and field trips. Destinations include Ireland, Egypt, Kenya, Indonesia, China, Morocco, Greece, Israel, Italy, Turkey, South Africa, Costa Rica, and more. If you are traveling alone and wish to share a room with another single traveler, you are guaranteed the double rate if you register 90 days in advance, even if a roommate is not found for you.

For information: TraveLearn, PO Box 315, Lakeville, PA 18438; 717-226-9114.

UNIVERSITY VACATIONS

Spend a week or more at a famous university in Europe, concentrating on a choice of subjects from the Legend of Camelot to the works of Jane Austen, Roman Britain, modern mystery writers, English operetta, radio astronomy, and the American Colonies. You'll stay on campus or in a first-class hotel, and attend lectures presented by university scholars, go on excursions to relevant locations, eat full breakfasts and four-course dinners. The participating universities include Oxford and Cambridge, in England; the University of Bologna, in Italy; the University of Leiden, in the Netherlands; Charles University, in Prague; the University of Paris-Sorbonne; and Harvard University, in Boston. Open to all ages, especially yours.

For information: University Vacations, 10461 NW 26th St., Miami, FL 33172; 800-792-0100 or 305-591-1736.

MORE WAYS TO GET SMARTER
CHAUTAUQUA INSTITUTION

For over a century people have been traveling up to the shores of Lake Chautauqua, in southwestern New York State, to a cultural summer center set in a Victorian village. The 856-acre hilltop complex offers a wide variety of educational programs, including summer weeks and off-season weekends designed for people over the age of 55. The 55-Plus Weekends and the Residential Week for Older Adults are filled up far in advance, so if you are interested, don't waste a moment before signing up.

Each 55-Plus Weekend has a specific focus, such as the U.S. Constitution, natural history, national politics, music appreciation, or trade relations with Japan. They include discussions, workshops, lectures, films, recreational activities, and evening entertainment, all led by professionals. Housing and meals are available in a residence hall with double rooms and shared baths.

The Residential Week for Older Adults is similar but longer. And it includes lodging and meals as well as admittance to other happenings at the center.

It's all quite cheap. The cost of tuition, room, meals, and planned activities for a Residential Week is currently $425, while a 55-Plus Weekend costs $25 for commuters or $125 if you want accommodations and meals.

For information: Program Center for Older Adults, Chautauqua, NY 14722; 800-836-ARTS or 716-357-6200.

CLOSE UP FOUNDATION

Close Up, in cooperation with AARP, invites thousands of older Americans to Washington, D.C., in the spring and fall, when the temperature is just right, for an insider's view of the government at work. Its goal is to help participants become more informed about current events, exchange views with political insiders and national leaders, attend exclusive seminars featuring public-policy experts, and take part in workshops designed to illustrate how public policy affects them and how they can affect it.

If you go, you'll spend extensive time on Capitol Hill, visit a foreign embassy, take study tours of monuments and museums, go to the theater, attend dinners, lodge in a comfortable hotel, and have some free time as well. Moderately priced, programs range from five days to a week and include lodging, meals, all activities and excursions. Programs are available to both individuals and groups.

About a dozen programs are offered every year in the spring and fall by this nonprofit nonpartisan organization that has now brought over 480,000 people of all ages to the capital city. Some of the programs emphasize history and take you to Colonial Williamsburg and Jamestown; others target the presidency and show you the presidential

AGE OF REASON WEB SITE

If you click on to this web site (http://www.ageofreason.com), you'll come upon more than 5,000 links to sites of interest for seniors. A nonprofit association, Age of Reason aims to promote the use of computers and the internet among those over 50. One of the several features of the site is its free Vacation and Home Exchange Directory that facilitates the exchange of hospitality in one another's homes and/or home-swapping vacations worldwide. Another is Pen Pals, which provides an e-mail directory of people who would like to correspond with others. And the Job Bank posts résumés for seniors seeking employment. You don't have to be a member to scan the web site and participate in the services, but you may join for $20 for two years and get a quarterly newsletter and special member benefits.

For information: Age of Reason, 2424 Danforth Ave., Toronto, ON M4C 1K9; e-mail, seniors@ageofreason.com.

homesteads; but the main focus always remains "inside" Washington.

The Congressional Senior Citizen Intern Program, developed by Close Up, is another way to get a first-hand look at the government. You may apply to be an intern and, if accepted, spend a week working with the congressional staff in the office of your own representative or senator.

For information: Close Up Foundation, 44 Canal Center Plaza, Alexandria, VA 22314; 800-363-4762 or 703-706-3668.

THE COLLEGE AT 60

Part of Fordham University and located at the Lincoln Center campus in New York City, the College at 60 offers credit courses in liberal arts subjects such as history, psychology, philosophy, economics, literature, music, art, and computers, taught by Fordham faculty members. Included are a lecture series and the use of all college facilities. After taking four seminars, students receive a certificate and are encouraged to enter the regular Fordham University program. Courses may be audited or taken for credit for fees that are half of the regular rates.

Believe it or not, you are eligible for the College at 60 when you are 50.

For information: The College at 60, Fordham University at Lincoln Center, 113 W. 60th St., Room 804, New York, NY 10023; 212-636-6740.

LEARNING ADVENTURES

The College of the Tehachapis, a community-based college without a campus, provides educational opportunities for its local constituency in and around California's Tehachapi Mountains, hosts many Elderhostel programs, and offers a series of its own low-cost 7- to 10-day educational senior programs in many settings. Open to anyone over the age of 50, the residential programs include, for example, a tour of Mexico's Copper Canyon, golf holidays in Bakersfield, backpacking in the Sierras, tennis camp, grandparent/grandkids camp, and a Spanish language program in Baja California. *For information:* COTT, PO Box 1911–61, Tehachapi, CA 93581; 805-823-8115.

NORTH CAROLINA CENTER FOR CREATIVE RETIREMENT

The NCCR involves more than 1,500 50-plus participants every year in its five-component program: the College for Seniors, in which members teach and learn together; a leadership for seniors program, which explores the history, civic life, and challenges of the community; two intergenerational mentoring programs—one matching retirees with university undergraduates, the other placing senior volunteers in area public schools; and a retirement relocation weekend program that covers everything from housing options to hiking trails in western North Carolina. *For information:* The North Carolina Center for Creative Retirement, 116 Rhodes Hall, University of North Carolina at Asheville, Asheville, NC 28804-3299; 704-251-6140.

NORTHEASTERN SENIOR SEMINARS

If you're 55 or older, you are eligible to enroll in a series of inexpensive one-week summer residential "campus vacations" at Skidmore College in upstate New York. You choose courses from a range of classes from economics to psychology to folk dancing, live in a dorm, and take part in activities on and off campus. If you like, you may enroll for two or three consecutive weeks with a different curriculum each week.

For information: Summer Special Programs, Skidmore College, Saratoga Springs, NY 12866-1632; 518-584-5000.

NEVER TOO LATE TO LEARN

SeniorNet is a nonprofit organization dedicated to bringing computer technology to older adults so that they may enhance their lives and those of others. SeniorNet currently has 90 Learning Centers across the United States, staffed by volunteer instructors and coaches, all of whom are seniors themselves. It has been online for over 10 years and maintains large sites on America Online and the World Wide Web (http://www.seniornet.org). Annual membership is $35 ($40 for couples) and includes admission to Learning Centers; a free AOL start-up kit with special membership rates; a quarterly newsletter; and discounts on books, hardware, and software.

For information: SeniorNet, 1 Kearny St., San Francisco, CA 94108; 800-747-6848.

OASIS

OASIS (Older Adult Service and Information System) is a nonprofit organization sponsored by the May Department Stores Company in collaboration with local hospitals, medical centers, government agencies, and other participants in about 40 locations across the nation. Its purpose is to enrich the lives of people over 55 by providing educational and wellness programs and volunteer opportunities to its

members. At its centers, OASIS offers classes ranging from French conversation and the visual arts to dance, bridge, creative writing, history, exercise, classical music, points of law, and prevention of osteoporosis. Also featured are special events such as concerts, plays, and museum exhibits; lectures; and even trips and cruises. If you live in an OASIS city, sign up—this is a good deal. Membership is free.
For information: The OASIS Institute, 7710 Carondelet Ave., Ste. 125, St. Louis, MO 63105; 314-862-2933.

PLUS PROGRAM, NYU

All students over 65 who register for courses in the School of Continuing Education at New York University are eligible to become members of PLUS, a Program of Lifelong Learning for University Seniors, for an additional fee of $75 per semester. Membership includes a choice of two specially designed, five-session mini-courses on a broad range of subjects. Topics for the courses, scheduled on Monday, Tuesday, and Thursday afternoons, have recently included Great Decisions in Foreign Policy, Contemporary Russian Humor, Visual Literacy, and the Genius of George Balanchine. PLUS members may also attend five weekly luncheon/discussion lectures with prominent speakers.
For information: PLUS, NYU School of Continuing Education, 11 W. 42nd St., New York, NY 10036; 212-790-1352 or 212-998-7130.

SENIOR SUMMER SCHOOL

Now you can go to college next summer, taking courses in subjects you've always wanted to know more about, while living in private or university residential halls for 2 to 10 weeks. Senior Summer School offers programs on your choice of six campuses: the University of Wisconsin, the University of California at Santa Barbara, San Diego State University, the University of Maine in Bangor, the University of Judaism in Los Angeles, and Mt. Allison University in New Brunswick, Canada. You choose your own curriculum. The courses are college-level, but there are no marks, grades, compulsory papers, or mandatory attendance requirements. Included in the programs are all meals, weekly housekeeping, excursions, and social activities. A mix of couples and singles, senior students include those who never finished high school as well as those with college and postgraduate degrees.

For information: Senior Summer School, PO Box 4424, Deerfield Beach, FL 33442-4424; 800-847-2466.

INSTITUTES FOR LEARNING IN RETIREMENT

Today there are about 200 community-based Institutes for Learning in Retirement throughout the U.S. and Canada that provide college-level courses on a noncredit basis for older adults. Each institute is sponsored by a college or university as a center for intellectual and social activity for its participants who are involved in determining curriculum, recruiting new members, and developing social programs.

In most cases, there are no tests or grades, although there may be assigned reading or other preparation. Students pay a modest annual membership fee and may usually take as many courses as they wish. At some institutions, they may take some regular undergraduate or adult education courses as well.

The following is a sampling of the learning programs. For a longer list and information about starting a new program, contact the Elderhostel Institute Network, an association of independent ILRs whose purpose is to extend the concept to new communities.

For information: Elderhostel Institute Network, 56 Dover Rd., Durham, NH 03824; 602-862-0725.

ACADEMY OF LIFELONG LEARNING

For information: University of Delaware, 2800 Pennsylvania Ave., CED, Wilmington, DE 19806; 302-573-4433.

DONOVAN SCHOLARS PROGRAM

A study program at the University of Kentucky in Lexington and at the 14 community colleges in Kentucky, the Donovan Scholars Program was designed specifically for students over the age of 65. It provides free tuition in all undergraduate or graduate courses in all academic areas. In addition, there are special noncredit course offerings for those over 60 in such subjects as art, music appreciation, radio drama, and exercise. Discussion groups meet twice a week and an annual week-long writing workshop (for people over 57) is held every summer.

For information: Donovan Scholars Program, Ligon House, University of Kentucky, Lexington, KY 40506-0442; 606-257-2656.

DUKE INSTITUTE FOR LEARNING IN RETIREMENT

Here some of the classes are led by peers, while others are taught by university faculty and local professionals.

For information: Duke University, PO Box 90704, Durham, NC 27708; 919-684-2703.

THE HARVARD INSTITUTE FOR LEARNING IN RETIREMENT

For information: Harvard Institute for Learning in Retirement, 51 Brattle St., Cambridge, MA 02138; 617-495-4072.

THE INSTITUTE FOR LEARNING IN RETIREMENT

For information: The American University, Nebraska Hall, 4400 Massachusetts Ave. NW, Washington, DC 20016; 202-885-3920.

THE INSTITUTE FOR RETIRED PROFESSIONALS

This program, at the New School for Social Research in New York, was established in 1962, the first such program of its kind. As the granddaddy of them all, it has served as a pilot program for similar schools at other institutions. It offers its members—about 550 retired professionals—more than 70 study groups in subjects ranging from Great Decisions to Virginia Woolf to Highlights of Mathematics to European history. Members may also enroll in one regular daytime New School course each semester.

For information: Institute for Retired Professionals, New School for Social Research, 66 W. 12th St., Room 502, New York, NY 10011; 212-229-5682.

INSTITUTE OF NEW DIMENSIONS

This peer-learning school at three campuses of Palm Beach Community College offers retirees, for a small yearly fee, a choice of more than 160 courses a year plus individual lectures, special events, and an annual conference. Taught by volunteer faculty, the program is located on campuses in Lake Worth, Palm Beach Gardens, and West Palm Beach. *For information:* Institute of New Dimensions, 4200 Congress Ave., Lake Worth, FL 33461; 407-439-8186.

NOVA COLLEGE INSTITUTE FOR RETIRED PROFESSIONALS

For information: Nova College Institute for Retired Professionals, 3301 College Ave., Fort Lauderdale, FL 33314; 305-475-7337.

THE PLATO SOCIETY OF UCLA

For information: The Plato Society of UCLA, 1083 Gayley Ave., Los Angeles, CA 90024; 301-794-0231.

PROFESSIONALS AND EXECUTIVES IN RETIREMENT

For information: Hofstra University, 205 Davison Hall, Hempstead, NY 11550; 516-463-6919.

TEMPLE ASSOCIATION FOR RETIRED PROFESSIONALS

For information: Temple University, 1619 Walnut St., Philadelphia, PA 19103; 215-787-1505.

EDUCATION IN CANADA

Virtually every college and university in Canada gives free tuition to students over the age of 60 or 65, whether they attend classes part-time or full-time. Colleges of applied arts and technology generally offer postsecondary credit courses through their Departments of Continuing Education or Extension to seniors and charge only a few dollars per course. Aside from the nonexistent or low cost, seniors are treated just like the other students, have the same privileges, and must abide by the same regulations.

For information: Write to the registrar of the college you've chosen for information about its program or, for general information, to the Ministry of Colleges and Universities in your province.

NATIONAL ACADEMY OF OLDER CANADIANS

Based in Vancouver, the NAOC's mission is to involve older Canadians in lifelong learning and to work in partnership with other nonprofit organizations to develop programs to promote its membership's contribution to society. These programs currently include computer classes, business training, workshops, learning circles, mentoring, town meetings, and discussion groups on issues of special interest. Annual membership fee is $20.

For information: National Academy of Older Canadians, 411 Dunsmuir St., Vancouver, BC V6B 1X4; 604-681-3767.

17

Shopping Breaks, Taxes, Insurance, and Other Practical Matters

This chapter is not filled with great suggestions for having fun. However, the information here may be very useful, alerting you to some facts you didn't know as well as benefits that are coming your way simply because you've lived so long.

SAVING MONEY IN THE STORES

All over the country, retail stores are now offering discounts to seniors because they realize that members of the mature population are cautious consumers who know the value of a dollar and are also extremely fond of good deals. In fact, the older population has now started to expect them.

Stores vary on the age you must be to receive their special offers, but most start you off at 60. Some give you 10 or 15 percent off every day, while others reserve one day a week for their senior discounts. Sometimes, however, instead of discounts, they advertise senior specials. Sears and Montgomery Ward, on the other hand, have clubs to join that entitle you to special discounts and other services.

MONTGOMERY WARD

Montgomery Ward's Y.E.S. (Years of Extra Savings) Discount Club saves you money in many ways when you've reached the age of 55. As a member, you receive a membership card and a bimonthly magazine called *Vantage*. The membership fee is currently $3.49 per month or $34.99 a year for you and your spouse. With the membership card in hand, you will get 10 percent off any merchandise, sale or nonsale, in all 350 Montgomery Ward stores every Tuesday. On Tuesdays, Wednesdays, and Thursdays, you're entitled to 10 percent off any auto labor charges. And there are other benefits, such as a pharmaceutical service.

What's more, the Y.E.S. Club Travel Service plans your travel, makes reservations, and gives you discounted prices plus cash rebates on the cost of your trips. This means that upon your return you will receive a check for a 10 percent rebate on all lodging and car rentals, and 5 percent on tours, cruises, rail passes, and airline tickets.

For information: Montgomery Ward Y.E.S. Discount Club, 200 N. Martingale Rd., Schaumburg, IL 60173; 800-421-5396.

SEARS

Sears started Mature Outlook many years ago as an over-50 club. Along with the club's other benefits, it offers savings to members when they cash in special discount coupons good for a variety of products and services. The coupons come your way regularly with an excellent magazine after you join the club and may be used in Sears stores in the United States and Canada. See Chapter 19 for more about Mature Outlook.

For information: Mature Outlook, PO Box 10448, Des Moines, IA 50306-0448; 800-336-6330.

FEDERAL INCOME TAXES

The tax laws no longer provide an extra exemption for people over the age of 65. Instead, they give you a larger standard deduction than younger people are entitled to, according to Julian Block, a Larchmont, NY, tax attorney and author of a popular guide to saving on income taxes, *Julian Block's Tax Avoidance Secrets.* You can ask him questions about your taxes by taking part in his chat room for income tax strategies on Prodigy, Monday nights at 10:30 P.M. EST.

The standard deductions for everyone *under* 65 for 1997 returns are $6,900 for married couples filing jointly; $3,450 each for married people filing separately; $4,150 for single people, and $6,050 for heads of households. These standard deductions change every year to reflect inflation, so be sure to check them out for each year's return.

If one spouse of a couple filing jointly is *over* 65, the standard deduction is increased for 1997 returns (by $800) to $7,700. If both members of a married couple are over 65, it is increased (by $800 twice) to $8,500.

For a married person over 65 filing separately, the deduction increases (by $800) to $4,250. A single person over 65 may deduct $5,150 ($1,000 more than those who are younger). And a head of household over 65 gets a standard deduction in 1997 of $7,050 ($1,000 more than an under-65).

None of these figures apply, of course, if you itemize your deductions. Remember that at age 65 you needn't file returns at all when your reportable income is below the amount required for filing.

By the way, the Internal Revenue Service issues a free booklet, *Tax Information for Older Americans* (Publication No. 554), which you can get at your local IRS office or by calling 800-TAX-FORM. You may also want to ask for its free *Guide to Free Tax Services* (Publication No. 910), which provides a list of IRS booklets on federal taxes and explains what each one covers. Request large-print tax forms if you need them.

SALE OF PRINCIPAL RESIDENCE

You can save money on taxes if you or your spouse is 55 when you sell the home you have owned and lived in as a principal residence for at least three years out of the five years leading up to the date of the sale. You may elect to exclude from your income for federal tax purposes up to $125,000 if you are single or married and filing a joint return. You may exclude $62,500 each if you are married and filing separately.

As much as $250,000 can be tax-free on the sale of a residence owned jointly by individuals who are not husband and wife—for example, a parent and child, a brother and sister, or an unmarried couple sharing quarters. As long as each unmarried joint owner is over 55, each gets to exclude up to $125,000 of his or her share of the profit. But when one is under 55 and the other over 55, only the older owner is eligible for the tax break.

Before you decide to take advantage of this, however, be sure to discuss it with a tax consultant. This is a once-in-a-lifetime opportunity and you may be better off saving the privilege for a later home sale.

HOW TO GET HELP WITH YOUR TAX RETURN

Assistance in preparing your tax returns is available free from both the Internal Revenue Service and AARP. The IRS offers Tax Counseling for the Elderly (TCE) for people over 60 and Voluntary Income Tax Assistants (VITA) for younger people who need help. Trained volunteers provide information and will prepare returns at thousands of sites throughout the country from February 2 to April 15. Watch your local newspaper for a list of sites in your area or call 800-TAX-1040 and press 0.

Or you may enlist the help of AARP's Tax-Aide Service where volunteers help low- and moderate-income members of AARP to prepare their tax returns from February 1 to April 15. To find the site nearest you, call AARP at 800-424-3410. Have your membership number and zip code handy and also your calendar, since an appointment is required.

AUTO AND HOMEOWNER'S INSURANCE

Mature people tend to be good drivers, much more careful than the younger crowd, having shed their bad habits such as speeding and reckless driving. And, although seniors total more accidents per mile, they drive fewer miles and usually don't use their cars for daily commuting. Therefore, statistically, they have fewer accidents per driver than other risk categories do, at least until they are very old. These are the reasons many insurance companies offer discounts on automobile coverage after you've reached a certain age, in most cases 55, and why they sometimes reduce them after age 70 or 75.

In addition, you may get a discount—usually 10 percent—on your automobile premiums in most states when you successfully complete a state-approved defensive-driving course. Among the programs is AARP's 55 Alive/Mature Driving, an eight-hour classroom refresher that specifically addresses the needs of older drivers with physical and perceptual changes that affect their driving. Open to both AARP members and nonmembers and taught by volunteers, the course is offered locally all over the country.

Some companies also offer reductions in premiums for homeowner's insurance, figuring you have become a cautious, reliable sort who takes good care of your property. Besides, you're likely to spend more time at home these days so you're around to keep your eye on things.

Although discounts are wonderful and we all love to get them, always shop the bottom line when you buy insurance; in other words, know what you are getting for what you are paying. If one company charges higher premiums for comparable coverage and then gives you a discount, you have not profited.

Insurance regulations differ from state to state, but here are some of the offerings made to older drivers and homeowners by some major insurance companies.

ALLSTATE

Allstate gives a discount of 10 percent off the premiums across the board—liability, comprehensive, and collision coverage—on automobile insurance in almost every state for those who are 55 and retired. And, in over 30 states, it takes an additional 5 or 10 percent off for graduates of an approved defensive-driving course. In Florida, things can get even better. Here drivers age 50 to 70 may apply for an additional 3 to 7 percent discount on top of the others.

As for homeowner property coverage, Allstate offers 10 percent off the premiums in most states to policyholders at age 55.

HOW TO SAVE YOUR LIFE

If you happen to get sick or have an accident while you're away from home, a nonprofit foundation called **MedicAlert** may save your health or even your life. When you join, at an annual fee of $15, you will receive a metal bracelet or neck chain engraved with your personal identification number and a 24-hour-a-day call-collect telephone number tied into a national data bank. When you or medical personnel call the data bank, all of your backup medical information is provided along with names and telephone numbers of your physician, next of kin, people to notify in an emergency, and other relevant information. As a backup, you get a wallet card with the same information. If you have an implanted medical device such as a pacemaker, heart valve, or breast implant, you may ask to be listed in MedicAlert's Implant Registry Service, which will alert you to recalls and safety information about your device.

For information: MedicAlert Foundation, PO Box 1009, Turlock, CA 95381; 800-ID-ALERT (800-432-5378).

AMERICAN FAMILY

If you are between the ages of 50 and 69, American Family gives you 10 percent off on almost all auto coverages. Preferred customers—those with good driving records—who buy both auto and homeowner insurance from this company get another 20 percent off. Not only that, but taking a defensive-driving course nets you an additional 5 to 10 percent discount in some states.

COLONIAL PENN

With this insurance company, you can save up to 10 percent on your automobile coverage if you are 55 or over and retired. Take a defensive-driving course and you'll save 10 percent more. You are guaranteed to get a policy renewal, regardless of your age or driving record, as long as you meet a few simple requirements, such as paying your premiums and maintaining a valid driver's license.

FARMERS

Policyholders over the age of 55 are offered discounts of 5 to 10 percent on automobile coverage in most states where Farmers Insurance is sold if they complete an approved defensive-driving course. A homeowner's credit starts at age 50 and ranges from 2 to 10 percent, depending on your age and the state in which you reside.

GEICO

In most states, GEICO offers good drivers between the ages of 50 and 74, retired or not, a lower rate on all automobile coverages on the cars they principally operate that are not used for business. A certificate from an accredited driving course may give you an additional 10 percent discount.

Over-50s are also eligible for a multirisk plan that gives them mechanical breakdown coverage on new cars in addition to comprehensive and collision coverages. Plus, a Prime Time contract, available in many states, adds a guarantee that your policy may not be canceled for reasons of age, accidents, or driving violations. For this, the principal operator of the household must be 50 or over, no one on the policy may be under 25, and all drivers cannot have had any accidents or violations for at least three years.

KEEP AN INVENTORY OF HOUSEHOLD GOODS

A free booklet, *Nonbusiness Disaster, Casualty and Theft Loss Workbook* (Publication No. 584), available from the Internal Revenue Service, is designed to help you determine the amount of a casualty or theft loss deduction for household goods and personal property. You use the booklet to list your possessions on a room-by-room basis, with space to record the number of items, date acquired, cost, value, and amount of loss. It is not easy to make a complete inventory of your possessions, but it is easier than trying to remember all those details after a theft or fire. Pick the booklet up at your local IRS office or call 800-TAX-FORM (800-829-3676).

ITT HARTFORD

The automobile and homeowner's insurance offered by AARP is underwritten by ITT Hartford, giving you a 10 percent discount for the next three years when you complete an accredited driving course and up to 5 percent for maintaining a safe driving record for three years. You are guaranteed not to have your policy canceled because of age.

On homeowner insurance in most states, Hartford allows up to 5 percent credit on the total premium at any age if you and your spouse are retired or work less than 24 hours a week.

NATIONWIDE

This company reduces premiums by 5 percent on all coverage from ages 50 to 54 in most states. From 55 to 59, you'll get a 10 percent discount; from 70 on, you get only a 5 percent reduction once more. Take a defensive-driving course and almost everywhere you'll be entitled to an additional 5 to 15 percent off.

PRUDENTIAL

Prudential gives drivers ages 50 through 54 a discount of about 10 percent in most states, 15 percent for ages 55 through 64, 10 percent for ages 65 through 74. You'll get an additional discount of 5 to 10 percent when you complete a defensive-driving course.

On homeowner insurance, there's a 5 percent Mature Homeowner Credit if one owner on the policy is 55 or more.

STATE FARM

Buy automobile insurance from State Farm and you'll get a 5 percent discount on certain coverages if you are 55 or more.

TRAVELERS

With this insurance company (now merged with Aetna's property and casualty division), the discount you get across the board on automobile coverage varies according to your age. From ages 50 through 64, the discount amounts to 10 to 15 percent depending on the state in which you live. From 65 through 74, it's 15 to 20 percent; and over 75, 5 to 10 percent. Completing a defensive-driving course will add another 5 percent discount in some states for those over 55. The vehicle must be used essentially for pleasure and no driver may be under 25 years of age.

On homeowner insurance, you will get 5 to 20 percent reductions on premiums, depending on the state, when you are 50 or more.

BANKING

Many banks offer special incentives and services to people over 55 or 60, ranging from free checking to free NOW accounts, elimination of savings-account fees, free insurance, travelers cheques, and safe-deposit boxes, and even cash rebates at restaurants. Every bank and every state is different, so you must check out the situation in your community. Do some careful comparison shopping to make sure you are getting the best deal available.

LEGAL ASSISTANCE

Call upon your local area senior agency, which is required by law to provide some legal assistance to older citizens. Yours may help you untangle some puzzling legal problems or, at least, tell you what services are available to you. Or contact the local bar association for information. It is quite possible that it operates a referral or pro bono program. Or, suggests the American Bar Association, ask your local Legal Services Program for help or referrals.

HOW TO FIND LOCAL ELDER SERVICES

For information about housing, home health services, adult day care centers, legal assistance, or other kinds of services for older people, call the Eldercare Locator at 800-677-1116. This nationwide governmental resource for elderly people or their caregivers will help you find an appropriate agency or program in your area. Call between 9 A.M. and 8 P.M. (Eastern Time) Monday through Friday and explain the problem. Be sure you know the name, address, and zip code of the person needing help.

18

Volunteer for Great Experiences

There's no need to let your talents and energy go to waste once you have stopped working for a living. If, perhaps for the first time in your life, you have hours to spare, maybe you'd like to spend some of them volunteering your services to organizations that could use your help. There is plenty of work waiting for you. If you are looking for a good match between your abilities and a program that needs them, consider the programs detailed here, all of them eager to take advantage of your years of experience.

But, first, keep in mind:

When you file your federal income tax, you are allowed to deduct unreimbursed expenses incurred while volunteering your services. These include transportation, parking, tolls, meals and lodging (in some cases), and uniforms.

AARP VOLUNTEER TALENT BANK

If you want to help others, get in touch with AARP's Volunteer Talent Bank program which puts people and work together. Many AARP programs are offered locally and conducted by volunteers in your own neighborhood. When you register, you'll be asked to complete a questionnaire about your experience, skills, and special interests, and this is matched with volunteer opportunities within the organization or by referral to other agencies in your community.

For information: To get the address of the AARP chapter nearest you, contact AARP Volunteer Talent Bank, 601 E St. NW, Washington, DC 20049; 800-424-3410 or 202-434-AARP.

ELDERHOSTEL SERVICE PROGRAMS

Elderhostel, the educational travel organization, offers an extensive Service Program that provides adults over the age of 55 opportunities for diverse volunteer projects all over the world. Work ranges from helping to build affordable housing to assisting in archeological digs, conducting environmental research, teaching English, and working with seriously ill children. Participants typically spend one to three weeks on the project of their choice, performing a variety of tasks, attending lectures and cultural events, visiting historical sites, and learning about the surrounding culture and environment. No prior experience or training is necessary. Most projects cost you little except your efforts to advance their goals.

The Elderhostel-sponsored programs are listed alphabetically below, along with other retirement volunteer opportunities.

CALIFORNIA STATE UNIVERSITY

At the university's programs in the San Bernardino National Forest, volunteers work with forest rangers on such projects as trail maintenance, wildlife surveys, revegetation tree marking, cutting and stacking brush, and repairing campgrounds.

For information: For a free catalog, write to Elderhostel Service Programs, PO Box 1959, Wakefield, MA 01880-5959; 617-426-7788.

CENTER FOR BIOACOUSTICS

Here, located near its parent organization, the Texas A&M University main campus, the Center for Bioacoustics studies North American landbird populations at its Central Flyway Bird Observatory. Register as a volunteer through Elderhostel and you can help collect data for its study of the effects on our birds of such environmental threats as habitat loss, climate change, and toxic pollution. You will help capture, measure, band, and release birds and conduct point counts at observation stations. At the same time, you will learn about avian biology and ecology.

For information: Elderhostel Service Programs, PO Box 1959, Wakefield, MA 01880-5959; 617-426-7788.

DOUBLE H HOLE IN THE WOODS

Double "H" Hole in the Woods Ranch, for critically ill and severely handicapped children, needs over-55 volunteers to help the children with swimming, boating, woodworking, creative arts, farming, music, nature studies, and more. Campers need support as they undergo therapy and receive treatment, and, not least, people to act as surrogate grandparents.

For information: Elderhostel Service Programs, PO Box 1959, Wakefield, MA 01880-5959; 617-426-7788.

EASTER SEALS CAMP

The Easter Seals Society of New Mexico offers a camp for people with physical or multiple disabilities, providing traditional camp experiences. Volunteers help in all aspects of camp activities, helping campers develop their skills, increase their self-esteem and independence, and adapt to their problems.

For information: Elderhostel Service Programs, PO Box 1959, Wakefield, MA 01880-5959; 617-426-7788.

FAMILY FRIENDS

A national program sponsored by the National Council on Aging, Family Friends recruits volunteers over the age of 55 to work with children with disabilities, chronic illnesses, or other problems in many locations around the country. The volunteers act as caring grandparents, helping the families in whatever ways they can, mostly dealing with children at home but occasionally in hospitals. They are asked to serve at least four hours a week and to commit themselves to the program for at least a year. Volunteers are reimbursed for expenses incurred.

The local projects are funded by the federal government, corporations, foundations, and local, county, city, or state governments.

For information: Family Friends Resource Center, 409 Third St. SW, Washington, DC 20024; 202-479-6675.

FOSTER GRANDPARENTS PROGRAM

This federal program sponsored by the government's national volunteer agency offers gratifying volunteer work to thousands of income-eligible men and women 60 and over, in communities all over the 50 states, Puerto Rico, the Virgin Islands, and the District of Columbia. The volunteers, who receive 40 hours of preservice orientation and training and four hours a month of in-service training, work with children who have special needs—boarder babies; troubled children; handicapped, severely retarded, abandoned, delinquent, abused, hospitalized, addicted, forlorn children who are desperate for love, care, and attention and do not get it from their families. Volunteers may work in hospitals, schools, homes, day-care programs, or residential centers.

HOW TO HELP THE ENVIRONMENT

Environmental Alliance for Senior Involvement (EASI) is designed to tap the talents, knowledge, experience, and enthusiasm of older environmental activists. Together with local and national senior and environmental organizations such as AARP, RSVP, the EPA, the National Council on Aging, World Wildlife Fund, and National Wildlife Federation, volunteers work to preserve and restore the natural world for future generations. Current projects include pollution control, water source protection, solar energy installations, and radon identification.

For information: EASI, 8733 Old Dumfries Rd., Catlett, VA 20119; 540-788-3274.

Volunteers, who must be in good health although they may be handicapped, work 20 hours a week. For this, they receive, aside from the immense satisfaction, a small tax-free annual stipend, a transportation allowance, hot meals while at work, accident and liability insurance, and annual physicals.

For information: Contact your local Foster Grandparents program, or the Corporation for National Service, 1201 New York Ave. NW, Washington, DC 20525; 800-424-8867 or 202-606-5000.

GLOBAL VOLUNTEERS

Founded with the goal of building a foundation for peace in the world through mutual understanding, Global Volunteers works on community development projects with host organizations year-round in many countries including the United States. Assigned to a team of volunteers of all ages and backgrounds, you work on projects such as preserving the rain forest in Costa Rica, renovating school facilities in Vietnam, and teaching English to children in Poland. You donate your time and pay your own way, and you need no professional experience in the project area. You may choose programs for one, two, or three weeks. Sign up via Elderhostel to join other 55-plus volunteers who are giving their time and effort to promote peace.

For information: Elderhostel Service Programs, PO Box 1959, Wakefield, MA 01880-5959; 617-426-7788.

HABITAT FOR HUMANITY

Among Elderhostel's many service programs is Habitat for Humanity, an ecumenical, nonprofit, Christian housing ministry that aims to eliminate poverty housing and homelessness by working side by side with homeowner families to build new homes or rehabilitate existing ones. Current locations are in small disadvantaged communities in the United States and abroad. Your contribution is your work and a small weekly donation designated for the purchase of building materials.

For information: Elderhostel Service Programs, PO Box 1959, Wakefield, MA 01880-5959; 617-426-7788.

INTERNATIONAL EXECUTIVE SERVICE CORPS

IESC, organized and directed by U.S. business executives, is a nonprofit organization that recruits retired, highly skilled executives and technical advisors in order to assist businesses in the developing nations. It is funded by the U.S. Agency for International Development (AID), overseas clients and foreign governments, and many American corporations.

After being briefed on the country and the client, volunteer executives travel overseas—with their spouses, if they wish—for projects that generally last two to three months. IESC pays for the couple's travel expenses and provides a per diem allowance.

For information: International Executive Service Corps, 333 Ludlow St., Stamford, CT 06902; 800-243-4372 or 203-967-6000.

NATIONAL EXECUTIVE SERVICE CORPS

This nonprofit organization performs a unique service: it helps other nonprofit organizations solve their problems by providing retired executives with extensive corporate and professional experience to serve as volunteer consultants. Its services are offered in five basic areas—education, health, the arts, social services, and religion—and the assistance covers everything from organizational structure and financial systems to marketing and funding strategy. Volunteers' expenses are covered.

For information: National Executive Service Corps, 257 Park Ave. South, New York, NY 10010; 212-529-6660.

NATIONAL PARK SERVICE

If you love the outdoors and have the time, volunteer to work for the National Park Service as a VIP (Volunteers in Parks). VIPs are not limited to over-50s, but a good portion of them are retired people with time, expertise, talent, and interest in forests and wilderness. You may work a few hours a week or a month, seasonally or full-time, and may or may not—depending on the park—wear a uniform or get reimbursed for out-of-pocket expenses. The job possibilities range from working at an information desk to serving as a guide, maintaining trails, driving a shuttle bus, painting fences, designing computer programs, patrolling trails, making wildlife counts, writing visitor brochures, and preparing park events.

For information: Contact the VIP coordinator at the national park where you would like to volunteer and request an application. Or, for addresses, contact the appropriate National Park Service regional office.

NORTHERN ARIZONA UNIVERSITY

Volunteers who sign up for work projects led by Northern Arizona University may choose to assist the staff in rescuing native plants at the Arboretum at Flagstaff, a high-elevation botanic garden. Or they may decide to help monitor plant and bird populations in Coconino National Forest, collect native plant seeds in the Grand Canyon, or work one-on-one with Navajo children in Monument Valley on improving their basic skills.

For information: Elderhostel Service Programs, PO Box 1959, Wakefield MA 01880-5959; 617-426-7788.

OCEANIC SOCIETY EXPEDITIONS

OSE organizes environmental field research expeditions in an effort to protect aquatic habitats and promote environmental education all over the world. Volunteers make observations, gather and analyze data, and help implement the goals of each project. Current sites include archaeological excavation and artifact cataloging in Belize; observing the behavior of black howler monkeys, also in Belize; collecting information on the ecology of Amazon River dolphins in Peru; and identifying humpback whales in Costa Rican waters.

For information: Elderhostel Service Programs, PO Box 1959, Wakefield, MA 01880-5959; 617-426-7788.

PEACE CORPS

No doubt you've always thought the Peace Corps was reserved for young idealists who have just graduated from college. The truth is that it's a viable choice for idealists of any age. Eighty is the upper age limit for acceptance into the Peace Corps, and since its beginning in 1961 thousands of Senior Volunteers have brought their talents and experience to almost 100 countries in Latin America, the Caribbean, Central and Eastern Europe, Africa, Asia, and the Pacific. To become a Senior Volunteer, you must be a

U.S. citizen and meet basic legal and medical criteria. Some assignments require a college or technical-school degree or an experience equivalent. Married couples are eligible and will be assigned together. Service is typically for two years.

What you get in return is the chance to travel, an unforgettable living experience in a foreign land, basic expenses, and housing, plus technical, language, and cultural training. You'll also have a chance to use your expertise constructively in fields such as agriculture, engineering, math/science, home economics, education, skilled trades, forestry and fisheries, and community development.

For information: Peace Corps, 1990 K St. NW, Washington, DC 20526; 800-424-8580.

RSVP (RETIRED AND SENIOR VOLUNTEER PROGRAM)

RSVP, an organization that receives funding, support, and technical assistance from the Corporation for National Service, the federal domestic volunteer agency, and functions under the auspices of local service organizations, matches the interests and abilities of men and women over 55 with part-time volunteer opportunities in their own communities. RSVP volunteers may be assigned to work in schools, libraries, courts, day-care centers, crisis centers, hospitals, nursing homes, or economic development agencies. You may get involved in tax aid, home repair, counseling, refugee assistance, home visitation, adult education, or whatever other services are needed in your area. You will serve without pay but may be reimbursed for or provided with transportation and other expenses. You may work for only several hours a week or many more than that if you wish.

For information: Contact your local or regional RSVP office or Corporation for National Service, 1201 New York Ave. NW, Washington, DC 20525; 800-424-8867 or 202-606-5000.

FORTY PLUS CLUBS

Offices in 20 cities throughout the United States comprise this nonprofit cooperative of unemployed executives, managers, and professionals, men and women, 40 years of age or more. Their objective is to help members conduct effective job searches and find new jobs. There is no paid staff. The members do all the work and help pay expenses with their one-time charge of $500 plus $100 per month thereafter. They must commit themselves to attend weekly meetings and spend at least two days a week working at the club and assisting others in their search for work.

In return, members are helped to examine their career skills and define their goals, counseled on résumé writing and interview skills, helped to plan marketing strategy, and given job leads. They may also use the club as a base of operations, with phone answering and mail service, computers, and reference library.

Forty Plus Clubs exist at this writing in New York City and Buffalo, New York; Oakland, San Diego, San Jose, and Los Angeles (with a branch in Laguna Hills), California; Lakewood, Colorado; Columbus, Ohio; Dallas and Houston, Texas; Murray, Ogden, and Provo, Utah; Philadelphia, Pennsylvania; Bellevue, Washington; Washington, D.C.; St. Paul, Minnesota; and Honolulu, Hawaii.

For information: Addresses of the clubs and descriptive material are available from Forty Plus of New York, 15 Park Row, New York, NY 10038; 212-233-6086.

SENIOR COMPANIONS

Senior Companions are income-eligible Americans 60 or over who volunteer four hours a day, five days a week, to provide services and companionship for the homebound, helping them maintain their independence. In a program funded and supported by the Corporation for National Service and by local agencies, the volunteers help other people cope with life. For example, they assist disabled veterans, recovering mental patients, Alzheimer's patients, the blind, recovering substance abusers, men and women recuperating from major surgery or illnesses, and those who are in chronic frail health.

Although the volunteers are not paid, they receive a modest nontaxable stipend that does not affect Social Security eligibility, reimbursement for transportation and meals, on-duty insurance, and an annual physical exam.

For information: Corporation for National Service, 1201 New York Ave. NW, Washington, DC 20525; 800-424-8867 or 202-606-5000.

SENIOR ENVIRONMENTAL EMPLOYMENT PROGRAM (SEE)

The SEE Program, administered by the Environmental Protection Agency (EPA), establishes grants to private non-profit organizations to recruit, hire, and pay experienced people over the age of 55 to help fight environmental problems. The recruits, who work part-time or full-time in EPA offices or in the field, are paid by the hour in jobs ranging from secretarial and clerical work to highly specialized positions. All are designed to assist the agency in protecting the environment and cleaning up America.

For information: Contact your regional EPA office or SEE Program, EPA, 401 M St. SW, Washington, DC 20460; 202-260-2574.

JOB PROGRAM FOR OLDER WORKERS

Senior Community Service Employment Program (SCSEP), a federally funded program, recruits unemployed low-income men and women over the age of 55, assesses their employment strengths, and hires them for paid jobs in community-service positions. At the same time, the enrollees begin training in new job skills, receive such help as counseling, physical examinations, group meetings, and job fairs while the agency tries to match them with permanent jobs in the private sector. If you qualify and are looking for a paying position, this agency is worth a try.

For information: SCSEP, National Council on the Aging, 409 Third St. SW, Washington, DC 20024; 202-479-1200. Or contact your local, county, or state Office for the Aging.

THE SERVICE CORPS OF RETIRED EXECUTIVES

SCORE is a national organization of both active and retired professionals and business executives who offer their expertise free of charge to small businesses. SCORE counselors, who include lawyers, business executives, accountants, engineers, managers, journalists, and other specialists, provide management assistance and advice to small-business people who are going into business or who are already in business but need expert help.

With a current membership of more than 12,000 men and women, SCORE has about 750 counseling locations all over the mainland United States as well as Puerto Rico, Guam, and the Virgin Islands. Funded and coordinated by the government's Small Business Administration, it is operated and administered by a staff and an elected board of volunteers.

For information: Contact your local U.S. Small Business Administration office or SCORE, 409 Third St. SW, 4th floor, Washington, DC 20416; 800-634-0245 or 202-205-6762.

SERVICE OPPORTUNITIES FOR OLDER PEOPLE (SOOP)

SOOP, sponsored by the Mennonite Association for Retired Persons and the Mennonite Board of Missions, provides a way for older people to contribute their experience and skills in a variety of locations throughout the U.S. and Canada. You may sign up for two weeks or up to a year, living at the site and working to help others in need in whatever way you can, from teaching, building, and child care to homemaking, farming, and administering. Once you decide on the kind of work and time commitment you prefer, you make plans with a location coordinator for your assignment and housing. Volunteers pay for their own travel, food, and lodging.

For information: Mennonite Board of Missions, PO Box 370, Elkhart, IN 46515; 219-294-7523.

SHEPHERD'S CENTERS OF AMERICA (SCA)

An interfaith, nonprofit organization of older adults who volunteer their skills to help seniors in their communities,

SCA has 87 centers in 26 states and one in Canada. Supported by Catholic, Jewish, and Protestant congregations as well as businesses and foundations, the centers operate many programs designed to enable older people to remain in their own homes as active participants in community life. They also encourage intergenerational interaction. Centers offer such in-home services as Telephone Visitors, Family Friends, Meals on Wheels, Handyhands Service, and Respite Care, all provided mostly by volunteers. Programs at the centers include other services, day trips, classes and courses as well as support groups and referrals. Membership is open to anyone over the age of 55.

For information: Shepherd's Centers of America, 6700 Troost Ave., Suite 616, Kansas City, MO 64131; 800-547-7073 or 816-523-1080.

VOLUNTEER GRANDPARENTS SOCIETY

The objective of this nonprofit organization in Canada is to match volunteer grandparents with families with children between the ages of 3 and 12 who have no accessible grandparents. The volunteers, who are not paid and do not commit to a contract or specific hours, establish a relationship of mutual enjoyment, support, and caring and become part of an extended family. Applicants are interviewed and carefully screened, and matches are based on compatibility as well as on geographic proximity. The organization, which originated in 1973 in Vancouver, has expanded into other areas in the province of British Columbia and serves as a model for similar agencies in Ottawa and Toronto.

For information: Volunteer Grandparents, #3, 1734 W. Broadway, Vancouver, BC V6J 1Y1.

FOR JOB HUNTERS

If you're over 40 and in the market for a job but don't know where to start looking for one, hook up with Operation ABLE, a nonprofit organization affiliated with agencies that will help match you with a likely employer. You're in luck if you live in Chicago, where there are four regional offices. In addition, there is a network of independent ABLE-like organizations, modeled after the original, in several other cities, including New York, Boston, Denver, Los Angeles, Atlanta, Seattle, and Little Rock.

Operation ABLE tries every which way to get you into the working world. It provides job counseling, on-the-job training, group training activities, and individual career assessment and guidance; teaches job-hunting skills; matches older workers with employers; operates a pool of temporaries; and offers myriad other services.
For information: Operation ABLE, 180 N. Wabash Ave., Chicago, IL 60601; 312-782-3335.

VOLUNTEERS IN TECHNICAL ASSISTANCE

VITA provides another avenue for helping developing countries. A nonprofit international organization, VITA provides volunteer experts who respond—usually by direct correspondence—to technical inquiries from people in these nations who need assistance in such areas as small-business development, energy applications, agriculture, reforestation, water supply and sanitation, and low-cost housing. Its volunteers also perform other services such as project planning, translations, publications, marketing strategies, evaluations, and technical reports and often become on-site consultants.

There is no minimum age, but you must be retired to serve. If you become a volunteer, you will not be paid, but you will be reimbursed for your travel and living expenses. *For information:* Volunteers in Technical Assistance, 1600 Wilson Blvd., Ste. 500, Arlington, VA 22209; 703-276-1800.

VOLUNTEER PROGRAMS IN ISRAEL

ACTIVE RETIREES IN ISRAEL (ARI)

Sponsored by B'nai B'rith International, ARI is a volunteer work program for people who are 50, in good health, and members of B'nai B'rith. Volunteers pay for the opportunity to live in the resort city of Netanya and work in the mornings for one or two months in hospitals, forests, kibbutzim, schools, and facilities for the elderly and the handicapped. Afternoons are spent learning Hebrew, while the evenings include concerts, discussion groups, and cultural activities. Guided tours of the country are part of the program. Optional trips to Eilat are available as add-ons to your stay. *For information:* ARI, B'nai B'rith Israel Commission, 1640 Rhode Island Ave. NW, Washington, DC 20036; 800-500-6533 or 202-857-6580.

JEWISH NATIONAL FUND

To qualify for the JNF Canadian American–Active Retirees in Israel, a two-month winter program sponsored by the Jewish National Fund, you must be over 50 and in good enough shape to work. Your first month will be spent working five mornings a week, tending the JNF national forests and, in addition, working at a choice of other jobs. Some volunteers choose to contribute their time in schools, hospitals, homes for the aged, army bases, universities, or kibbutzim, while others assist local craftspeople or archaeologists. Afternoons are devoted to planned activities, including Hebrew lessons, and evenings are devoted to socializing. For your second month, you'll tour the country and spend time in Jerusalem.

For information: JNF CA-ARI Program, Missions Dept., 42 E. 69th St., New York, NY 10021; 800-223-7787 or 212-879-9300.

VOLUNTEERS FOR ISRAEL

In this volunteer work-and-cultural program for adults 18 and older in Israel, you'll put in eight-hour days for three weeks, sleep in a segregated dormitory, and work in small groups at a reserve or supply military base, doing whatever needs doing most at that moment. You may serve in supply, warehousing, or maintenance of equipment or in social services in hospitals. You'll wear an army uniform with a "Civilian Volunteer" patch. Board, room, and other expenses are free, but you must pay for your own partially subsidized airfare.

For information: Volunteers for Israel, 330 West 42nd St., 16th floor, New York, NY 10036-6902; 212-643-4848.

WINTER AND SPRING IN NETANYA PROGRAMS

Hadassah's Winter in Netanya (WIN) and Springtime in Netanya (SPIN) programs send volunteers to Israel for one or two months to work, study, and absorb Israeli culture. For a month in December, for two months in January and February, or for a month in the spring, American participants live in a four-star hotel in Netanya, a Mediterranean resort town 20 miles north of Tel Aviv. Here the volunteer workers, most of them retirees, spend their mornings working at the local hospital, tutoring schoolchildren in English, packing supplies for the Israel Defense Forces, pruning and planting trees, visiting senior centers, painting murals, or doing carpentry. Afternoons are devoted to optional Hebrew lessons and sightseeing tours, while evenings are reserved for social and cultural events.

For information: Hadassah, 50 West 58th St., New York, NY 10019; 212-303-8133 or your local Hadassah chapter.

AARP WORKS

A series of eight job-search workshops on employment planning, AARP Works is now offered year-round throughout the country. Led by AARP volunteer teams and community agencies, the workshops help midlife and older job seekers to identify and redefine their skills, interests, and work experience; explore ways to overcome obstacles to employment, such as age discrimination; and learn effective job-search techniques. A fee of $20 is charged for materials.

For information: For locations and dates, contact your local AARP area office. To find out where your area office is located, call AARP at 800-424-3410.

19

The Over-50 Organizations and What They Can Do for You

When you consider that there are more people in this country over the age of 55 than there are children in elementary and high schools, you can see why we have powerful potential to influence what goes on around here. As the demographic discovery of the decade, a group that controls most of the nation's disposable income, we've become an enormous marketing target. And, just like any other group of people, we've got plenty of needs.

A number of organizations in the United States and Canada have been formed in recent years to act as advocates for the mature population and to provide us with special programs and services. Here is a brief rundown on them and what they have to offer you. You may want to join more than one of them so you may get the best of each.

AARP (AMERICAN ASSOCIATION OF RETIRED PERSONS)

At age 50 you are eligible to join AARP, the extensive non-profit organization that serves as an advocate for the older generation and offers a vast array of services and programs. With more than 35 million members, it is one of the most effective lobbying groups in the country. You do not have to be retired to join. Its newsletter *AARP Bulletin* and magazine *Modern Maturity* go to more homes than any other publication in the U.S. For an annual membership fee of $8 (and that includes a spouse), AARP offers so many benefits that you are likely to stop reading before the end of the list. But here are some of them:

- Group health insurance; life insurance; auto insurance; homeowner's insurance; mobile-home insurance
- Discounts on hotels, motels, auto rentals, and sight-seeing
- A mail-order pharmacy service that delivers prescription and nonprescription drugs
- A motoring plan that includes emergency road and towing services, trip planning, and other benefits
- A national advocacy and lobbying program at all levels of government to develop legislative priorities and represent the interests of older people
- More than 4,000 local chapters with their own activities and volunteer projects
- The Volunteer Talent Bank that matches you with volunteer opportunities in your community
- A series of employment planning workshops called AARP Works for older jobhunters

■ Special programs in a wide range of areas such as consumer affairs, legal counseling, financial information, housing, health advocacy, voter education, employment planning, independent living, disability initiatives, grandparent information, and public benefits

■ Tax-Aide, a program conducted in cooperation with the IRS, that helps lower- and moderate-income members with their income tax returns

■ 55 ALIVE/Mature Driving, a classroom course developed to refresh your driving skills and in many states help you qualify for lower auto insurance rates

■ Free publications on many subjects relevant to your life.

For information: AARP, 601 E St. NW, Washington, DC 20049; 800-424-3410 or 202-434-AARP.

CANADIAN ASSOCIATION OF RETIRED PERSONS

You and your spouse may join CARP, a national nonprofit association of 230,000 Canadians over 50, retired or not, for $10 (Canadian) a year or $25 for three years. U.S. residents may join for $20 (Canadian) a year. Like AARP, this organization offers you discount rates on many good things, such as hotel rooms, car rentals, out-of-country health insurance, car, home and other insurance plans, and special travel discounts. It publishes a lively and informative newspaper six times a year and sponsors national and provincial advocacy programs on issues of concern to older people. Look for CARP's financial planning and other informative seminars held frequently throughout the country. *For information:* CARP, 27 Queen St., Ste. 1304, Toronto, ON M5C 2M6; 416-363-8748.

CANADIAN SNOWBIRD ASSOCIATION

CSA is an organization formed to represent the interests of Canadian snowbirds, people who flee the winter snow for the sun and palm trees of the U.S. southern states. As their advocate and lobbying group, CSA addresses issues of concern to Canadian seniors such as health care, absentee voting rights, cross-border problems, residency requirements, U.S. tax laws for Canadians wintering abroad, and estate tax rules on Canadian-owned vacation property in the U.S. And it sells travel insurance as well as out-of-country health insurance.

Membership costs $10 (single) and $15 (couple) per year, and benefits include a bimonthly magazine, group travel offerings, an automobile club, a currency exchange program, mail-order pharmacy services, discounted prescriptions and telephone calls, discounts on Days Inns room rates, and social gatherings in popular snowbird locations such as Florida and Arizona.

For information: Canadian Snowbird Association, 180 Lesmill Rd., North York, ON M3B 2T5; 800-265-3200.

CATHOLIC GOLDEN AGE

A Catholic nonprofit organization that is concerned with issues affecting older citizens, such as health care, housing, and Social Security benefits, CGA has well over a million members and more than 200 chapters throughout the country. It offers many good things to its members who must be over 50. These include spiritual benefits, such as masses and prayers worldwide, and practical benefits, such as discounts on hotels, campgrounds, car rentals, and prescriptions. Other offerings include group insurance plans, pilgrimage and group travel programs, and an automobile

club. Membership costs $8 a year or $19 for three years.
For information: Catholic Golden Age, 430 Penn Ave.,
Scranton, PA 18503; 800-836-5699.

MATURE OUTLOOK

Sponsored by Sears, the country's largest retailer, Mature
Outlook is a discount club for people who have turned 50.
Its 750,000 members are entitled to discounts on products
and services in all Sears stores in the U.S. and Canada.
When you join for a membership fee of $14.95 a year (in-
cludes you and your spouse), you receive $100 in Sears
money coupons to spend as you like. Other benefits of
membership include half price on the regular room rates
at more than 3,000 hotels and motels; a dining plan that
can also save up to 50 percent in hundreds of restaurants
worldwide; travel discounts; up to 25 percent off on car
rentals from Budget, Hertz, Avis, Alamo, and National; and
reductions on the cost of eye examinations and eyeglasses.
In addition, you'll receive six issues a year of *Mature Outlook Magazine,* a good read that also keeps you informed
about upcoming opportunities for savings.
For information: Mature Outlook, PO Box 10448, Des
Moines, IA 50306-0448; 800-336-6330.

NATIONAL COUNCIL OF SENIOR CITIZENS

An advocacy organization, NCSC lobbies on the local, state,
and national level for legislation benefiting older Americans.
With about five million members, it has carried on many
campaigns concerning Medicare, housing, health care, Social Security, and other relevant programs.

Although NCSC's major focus is its legislative program,

it also has a local club network, social events, prescription discounts, group rates on supplemental health insurance, automobile insurance, and travel discounts, plus a newspaper that keeps you up to date on all of the above.

For information: National Council of Senior Citizens, 1331 F St. NW, Washington, DC 20004; 800-333-7212 or 202-347-8800.

NATIONAL ASSOCIATION FOR RETIRED CREDIT UNION PEOPLE

Obviously, not everybody can join this club, but those who do—past and present members of a credit union who are at least 50 years old or retired—will get some good benefits. These include a magazine called *Prime Times*, a newsletter, car-rental discounts, Medicare supplement insurance, pharmacy discounts, lodging discounts at some hotels and campgrounds, and a motor club. Also, discounted travel packages and tours.

For information: NARCUP, PO Box 391, Madison, WI 53701; 800-937-2644, ext. 6070, or 608-232-6070.

NATIONAL ASSOCIATION OF RETIRED FEDERAL EMPLOYEES

As you can probably gather, this is an association of federal retirees and their families. Its primary mission is to protect the earned benefits of retired federal employees via its lobbying program in Washington. Members receive a monthly magazine and are entitled to discounts and special services.

For information: NARFE, 1533 New Hampshire Ave. NW, Washington, DC 20036; 800-627-3394 or 202-234-0832.

OLDER WOMEN'S LEAGUE

OWL is a national nonprofit organization with local chapters dedicated to achieving economic, political, and social equality for older women. Anyone, any age, may join. OWL provides educational materials, training for citizen advocates, and informative publications dealing with the important issues—such as Social Security, health care, retirement benefits, employment discrimination—facing women as they grow older. Annual dues: $25.

For information: Older Women's League, 666 11th St. NW, Washington, DC 20001; 800-825-3695 or 202-783-6686.

NATIONAL ALLIANCE OF SENIOR CITIZENS

This national lobbying organization with over 100,000 members has a decidedly conservative tilt-to-the-right bias, so people with middle-of-the-road or liberal views would not feel too much at home here. It works to influence national policy "on key issues of great importance to America and her future." As a member you receive newsletters and benefits that include group insurance, prescription discounts, discounts on car rentals, lodgings, moving expenses, and an automobile club.

For information: National Alliance of Senior Citizens, 1744 Riggs Pl. NW, Washington, DC 20009; 202-986-0117.

GRAY PANTHERS

A national organization of intergenerational activists, the Gray Panthers work on multiple issues that include peace, jobs for all, antidiscrimination (ageism, sexism, racism), family security, environment, campaign reform, and the

United Nations. They are active in more than 50 local networks across the United States in their efforts to promote their goal of advancing social justice. For annual membership dues of $20, members receive a bi-monthly newsletter which is also available by subscription.

For information: Gray Panthers, 2025 Pennsylvania Ave. NW, Ste. 821, Washington, DC 20006; 800-280-5362 or 202-466-3132.

THE RETIRED OFFICERS ASSOCIATION

This group is open to anyone who has been a commissioned or warrant officer in the seven U.S. uniformed services. Members receive lobbying representation on Capitol Hill and a magazine featuring articles devoted to matters of special interest to them. They may also take advantage of a number of benefits, including discounts on car rentals and motel lodgings, a travel program with "military fares" to many overseas destinations, sports tournaments, a mail-order prescription program, group health and life insurance plans, and a car lease-purchase plan. TROA also has many autonomous local chapters with their own activities and membership fees.

For information: The Retired Officers Association, 201 N. Washington St., Alexandria, VA 22314-2539; 800-245-8762 or 703-549-2311.

UNITED SENIORS ASSOCIATION

United Seniors Association fights for "less government regulation and lower taxes" for seniors. Organized to help stop a national health care plan, its mission is to lobby Congress for its conservative agenda and to get its point of view known via the media, position papers, and a newsletter. Membership costs $5 a year per household.

For information: USA, Inc., 12500 Fair Lakes Circle, Ste. 125, Fairfax, VA 22033; 800-890-1166 or 703-803-6747.

Index